Disclaimer

The publisher of this book is by no way associated with the National Institute of Standards and Technology (NIST). The NIST did not publish this book. It was published by 50 page publications under the public domain license.

50 Page Publications.

Book Title: Information Technology Security Training Requirements: A Role- and Performance-Based Model

Book Author: Mark Wilson; D E. deZafra; S I. Pitcher; J D. Tressler; J B. Ippolito;

Book Abstract: This document supersedes NIST 500-172, Computer Security Training Guidelines, published in 1989. The new document supports the Computer Security Act (Public Law 100-235) and OMB Circular A-130 Appendix III requirements that NIST develop and issue computer security training guidance. This publication presents a new conceptual framework for providing information technology (IT) security training. This framework includes the IT security training requirements appropriate for today's distributed computing environment and provides flexibility for extension to accommodate future technologies and the related risk management decisions.

Citation: NIST SP - 800-16

Keyword: awareness;behavioral objectives;education;individual accountability;job function;management and technical controls;rules of behavior;training

NIST Special Publication 800-16

U.S. DEPARTMENT OF
COMMERCE
Technology Administration
National Institute of Standards
and Technology

Mark Wilson — Editor
Dorothea E. de Zafra
Sadie I. Pitcher
John D. Tressler
John B. Ippolito

Information Technology Security Training Requirements:
A Role- and Performance-Based Model

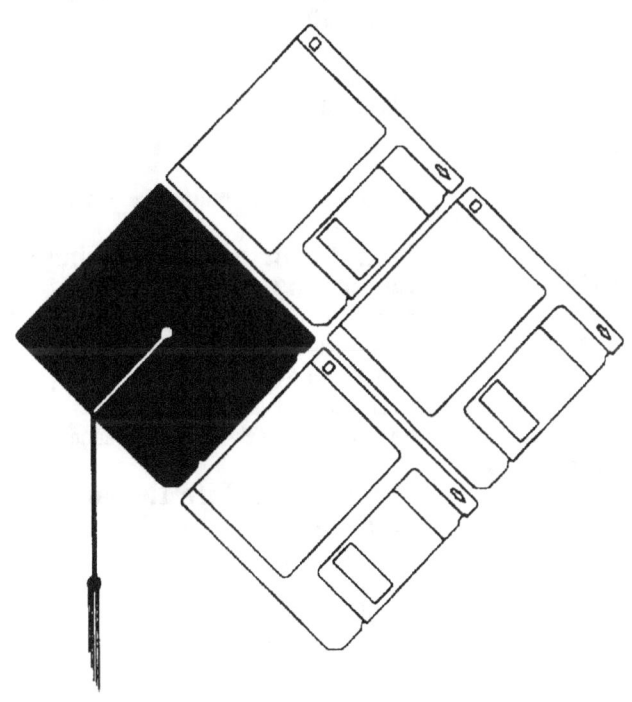

The National Institute of Standards and Technology was established in 1988 by Congress to "assist industry in the development of technology . . . needed to improve product quality, to modernize manufacturing processes, to ensure product reliability . . . and to facilitate rapid commercialization . . . of products based on new scientific discoveries."

NIST, originally founded as the National Bureau of Standards in 1901, works to strengthen U.S. industry's competitiveness; advance science and engineering; and improve public health, safety, and the environment. One of the agency's basic functions is to develop, maintain, and retain custody of the national standards of measurement, and provide the means and methods for comparing standards used in science, engineering, manufacturing, commerce, industry, and education with the standards adopted or recognized by the Federal Government.

As an agency of the U.S. Commerce Department's Technology Administration, NIST conducts basic and applied research in the physical sciences and engineering, and develops measurement techniques, test methods, standards, and related services. The Institute does generic and precompetitive work on new and advanced technologies. NIST's research facilities are located at Gaithersburg, MD 20899, and at Boulder, CO 80303. Major technical operating units and their principal activities are listed below. For more information contact the Publications and Program Inquiries Desk, 301-975-3058.

Office of the Director
- National Quality Program
- International and Academic Affairs

Technology Services
- Standards Services
- Technology Partnerships
- Measurement Services
- Technology Innovation
- Information Services

Advanced Technology Program
- Economic Assessment
- Information Technology and Applications
- Chemical and Biomedical Technology
- Materials and Manufacturing Technology
- Electronics and Photonics Technology

Manufacturing Extension Partnership Program
- Regional Programs
- National Programs
- Program Development

Electronics and Electrical Engineering Laboratory
- Microelectronics
- Law Enforcement Standards
- Electricity
- Semiconductor Electronics
- Electromagnetic Fields[1]
- Electromagnetic Technology[1]
- Optoelectronics[1]

Chemical Science and Technology Laboratory
- Biotechnology
- Physical and Chemical Properties[2]
- Analytical Chemistry
- Process Measurements
- Surface and Microanalysis Science

Physics Laboratory
- Electron and Optical Physics
- Atomic Physics
- Optical Technology
- Ionizing Radiation
- Time and Frequency[1]
- Quantum Physics[1]

Materials Science and Engineering Laboratory
- Intelligent Processing of Materials
- Ceramics
- Materials Reliability[1]
- Polymers
- Metallurgy
- NIST Center for Neutron Research

Manufacturing Engineering Laboratory
- Precision Engineering
- Automated Production Technology
- Intelligent Systems
- Fabrication Technology
- Manufacturing Systems Integration

Building and Fire Research Laboratory
- Structures
- Building Materials
- Building Environment
- Fire Safety Engineering
- Fire Science

Information Technology Laboratory
- Mathematical and Computational Sciences[2]
- Advanced Network Technologies
- Computer Security
- Information Access and User Interfaces
- High Performance Systems and Services
- Distributed Computing and Information Services
- Software Diagnostics and Conformance Testing

---

[1] At Boulder, CO 80303.
[2] Some elements at Boulder, CO.

NIST Special Publication 800-16   Information Technology Security Training Requirements:
A Role- and Performance-Based Model

Mark Wilson — Editor
Dorothea E. de Zafra
Sadie I. Pitcher
John D. Tressler
John B. Ippolito

COMPUTER SECURITY

Information Technology Laboratory

National Institute of Standards
and Technology
Gaithersburg, MD 20899-0001

Supersedes Special Publication 500-172

April 1998

U.S. Department of Commerce
William M. Daley, Secretary

Technology Administration
Gary R. Bachula, Acting Under Secretary for Technology

National Institute of Standards and Technology
Raymond G. Kammer, Director

Reports on Computer Systems Technology

The Information Technology Laboratory (ITL) at the National Institute of Standards and Technology (NIST) promotes the U.S. economy and public welfare by providing technical leadership for the Nation's measurement and standards infrastructure for information technology. ITL develops tests, test methods, reference data, proof of concept implementations and technical analyses to advance the development and productive use of information technology. ITL's responsibilities include the development of technical, physical, administrative, and management standards and guidelines for the cost-effective security and privacy of sensitive unclassified information in federal computer systems. This Special Publication 800 series reports on ITL's research, guidance, and outreach efforts in computer security, and its collaborative activities with industry, government, and academic organizations.

**National Institute of Standards and Technology Special Publication 800-16
Natl. Inst. Stand. Technol. Spec. Publ. 800-16, 200 pages (Apr. 1998)
CODEN: NSPUE2**

**U.S. GOVERNMENT PRINTING OFFICE
WASHINGTON: 1998**

For sale by the Superintendent of Documents, U.S. Government Printing Office, Washington, DC 20402

Information Technology Security Training Requirements

FOREWORD

In 1997 the General Accounting Office (GAO) identified information technology (IT) security as "a new high-risk area that touches virtually every major aspect of government operations" (report # GAO/HR-97-30). In doing so, GAO went beyond dozens of specific recommendations in its prior reports to identify underlying factors. Several are people factors, not technological factors, e.g., "insufficient awareness and understanding of information security risks among senior agency officials," "poorly designed and implemented security programs," "a shortage of personnel with the technical expertise needed to manage controls," and "limited oversight of agency practices."

The key to addressing people factors or competencies is awareness, training, and education. Certainly the need for government-wide attention to this area of IT security has never been greater, so issuance of this publication, *Information Technology Security Training Requirements: A Role- and Performance-Based Model,* (Training Requirements) is especially timely. This document has been designed as a "living handbook" to have the longest useful life possible as the foundation of and structure for "do-able" training by Federal agencies. To meet this objective, the following elements have been included in this document's design:

- Dates, references, or other items that would quickly outdate the Training Requirements have been excluded. Excluded also are "terms du jour" and items which may be specific to a given agency or Department. Technical jargon changes rapidly—even though the meanings are not significantly different. Thus, to avoid unnecessary outdating, the document uses terminology that is most consistent across Federal agencies and broadest in scope to encompass all information processing, storage, and transmission resources and technologies—for example, "Information Technology." A glossary of key terms is provided in an appendix.

- An extensible set of knowledges, skills, and abilities (KSAs) structure the Training Requirements and are linked to the document through *generic* IT Security Body of Knowledge, Topics and Concepts categories as shown in Exhibit 4-4. Thus, new technologies and associated terminology may be added to the KSAs (which are to be maintained in a separate database), and will be tracked forward through the generic IT Security Body of Knowledge, Topics and Concepts categorization to recommended instructional blocks defined in Chapter 4. This linkage precludes a need to continually revise or supersede the key chapter that addresses training criteria with respect to security requirements affected by the ongoing evolution of information technology.

- Finally, the emphasis of the Training Requirements is on training <u>criteria</u> or standards, rather than on specific curricula or content. The training criteria are established according to trainees' role(s) within their organizations, and are measured by their on-the-job performance. This emphasis on roles and results, rather than on fixed content, gives the Training Requirements flexibility, adaptability, and longevity.

Foreword

ACKNOWLEDGMENTS

NIST acknowledges the many people who assisted with the development of this document. We thank the members of the Federal Computer Security Program Managers' Forum and the Federal Information Systems Security Educators' Association (FISSEA), and in particular, the four members of the FISSEA working group who co-authored the document:

Ms. Dorothea E. de Zafra
Senior Program Analyst and Science Education Program Coordinator
National Institutes of Health
U.S. Department of Health and Human Services

Ms. Sadie I. Pitcher
Information Technology Security Manager (Retired)
U.S. Department of Commerce

Mr. John D. Tressler
Computer Security Officer
Office of the Deputy Chief Information Officer
U.S. Department of Education

Mr. John B. Ippolito
Director, IT Security Services
Allied Technology Group, Inc.

Several colleagues made special contributions to this final product, and the authors gratefully acknowledge their assistance: Ms. Kathie Everhart (NIST) served as the NIST Liaison during the first two years of this document's development and provided valuable contributions in such areas as the "Basics and Literacy" curriculum; Dr. W. Vic Maconachy (National Security Agency) took a lead role in the initial development of the learning continuum and served as the primary interface with the defense and intelligence communities; Ms. K Rudolph (Native Intelligence) provided critical subject matter knowledge, computer graphics skills, and editorial support in the formation of the final product; and finally, Dr. Roger Quane (National Security Agency) provided training evaluation expertise and was the primary author of Chapter 5.

NIST also thanks those who reviewed draft versions of this document. Their comments were significant in shaping the final document.

TABLE OF CONTENTS

Page

FOREWORD iii

ACKNOWLEDGMENTS iv

CHAPTER 1. INTRODUCTION 1
    1.1 Background 3
    1.2 Purpose 4
    1.3 Principles of the New Approach: Results-Based Learning 5
    1.4 Use of this Document 7
    1.5 Document Organization 7

CHAPTER 2. LEARNING CONTINUUM — MODEL AND OVERVIEW 11
    2.1 Introduction to the Model 13
    2.2 Levels of Learning 15
        2.2.1 Awareness 15
        2.2.2 Training 16
        2.2.3 Education 16
    2.3 Comparative Framework 17
    2.4 Learning Styles and Effective Teaching Methods 19
        2.4.1 Ways of Learning and Implications for Instruction 19
        2.4.2 Additional Considerations for Adult Learning 20
        2.4.3 References 21

CHAPTER 3. SECURITY BASICS AND LITERACY 23
    3.1 Definition and Purpose 25
    3.2 Basics — Core Set of IT Security Terms and Concepts 26
    3.3 Literacy — Curriculum Framework 32

CHAPTER 4. TRAINING DEVELOPMENT METHODOLOGY:
                  ROLE-BASED TRAINING 41
    4.1 Introduction 43
    4.2 IT Security Training Matrix Cells 55
        4.2.1 Training Area: Laws and Regulations 57
        4.2.2 Training Area: Security Program 71
        4.2.3 Training Area: System Life Cycle Security 93

TABLE OF CONTENTS (Continued)

Page

CHAPTER 5. EVALUATING TRAINING EFFECTIVENESS 155
    5.1 Value of Evaluation in a Training Program 157
    5.2 Purposes of Training Effectiveness Evaluation 158
    5.3 Development of an Evaluation Plan 158
        5.3.1 Behavioral Objectives 159
        5.3.2 Levels of Evaluation 160
    5.4 Implementation of Evaluation Planning 163
    5.5 Summary 170
    5.6 Chapter References 170

APPENDIX A — LEARNING CONTINUUM A-1
APPENDIX B — TRAINING MATRIX B-1
APPENDIX C — GLOSSARY C-1
APPENDIX D — SELECTED GOVERNMENT IT SECURITY REFERENCES D-1
APPENDIX E — JOB FUNCTION-TRAINING CROSS REFERENCE E-1

INDEX I-1

LIST OF EXHIBITS

Page

Exhibit 1-1, NIST SP 500-172 Training Matrix 4
Exhibit 1-2, Use of this Document 8
Exhibit 2-1, IT Security Learning Continuum 13
Exhibit 2-2, Comparative Framework 18
Exhibit 3-1, ABC's of Information Technology Security 27
Exhibit 3-2, IT Security ABC's—Terms and Concepts 28
Exhibit 4-1, IT Security Training Matrix 44
Exhibit 4-2, Cell Format 45
Exhibit 4-3, Frequency of Sample Job Function Occurrence 47
Exhibit 4-4, IT Security Body of Knowledge Topics and Concepts 48
Exhibit 5-1, Evaluation Objectives 164
Exhibit 5-2, Sample Questionnaire — Level 1 Evaluation Training Assessment by Student .. 165
Exhibit 5-3, Sample Questionnaire — Level 3 Evaluation Training Assessment by
   Supervisor 167
Exhibit 5-4, Correlation of Evaluation Elements 171

CHAPTER

1

INTRODUCTION

CHAPTER 1. INTRODUCTION

1.1 Background

Federal agencies and organizations cannot protect the integrity, confidentiality, and availability of information in today's highly networked systems environment without ensuring that each person involved understands their roles and responsibilities and is adequately trained to perform them. The human factor is so critical to success that the Computer Security Act of 1987 (Public Law [P.L.] 100-235) required that, *"Each agency shall provide for the mandatory periodic training in computer security awareness and accepted computer practices of all employees who are involved with the management, use, or operation of each Federal computer system within or under the supervision of that agency."*

In accordance with P.L. 100-235, the National Institute of Standards and Technology (NIST), working with the U.S. Office of Personnel Management (OPM), was charged with developing and issuing guidelines for Federal computer security training. This requirement was satisfied by NIST's issuance of *"Computer Security Training Guidelines"* (Special Publication [SP] 500-172) in November 1989. In January 1992, OPM issued a revision to the Federal personnel regulations which made these voluntary guidelines mandatory. This regulation, 5 CFR Part 930, is entitled *"Employees Responsible for the Management or Use of Federal Computer Systems"* and requires Federal agencies to provide training as set forth in NIST guidelines.

The OPM regulation requires training: for current employees; new employees within 60 days of hire; whenever there is a significant change in the agency's IT security environment or procedures, or when an employee enters a new position which deals with sensitive information; and periodically as refresher training, based on the sensitivity of the information the employee handles. Office of Management and Budget (OMB) Circular A-130, *"Management of Federal Information Resources,"* Appendix III, *"Security of Federal Automated Information Resources,"* re-emphasizes these mandatory training requirements. In addition, it requires that prior to being granted access to IT applications and systems, all individuals must receive specialized training focusing on their IT security responsibilities and established system rules.

The NIST guidelines in SP 500-172 provided a framework for determining the training needs of particular categories of employees (including contractors) involved with sensitive but unclassified computer systems. The framework reflected the late 1980's when the IT environment was mainframe oriented. The focal point of SP 500-172 is its Training Matrix, shown on the following page as Exhibit 1-1.

Information Technology Security Training Requirements

**Exhibit 1-1
NIST SP 500-172 Training Matrix**

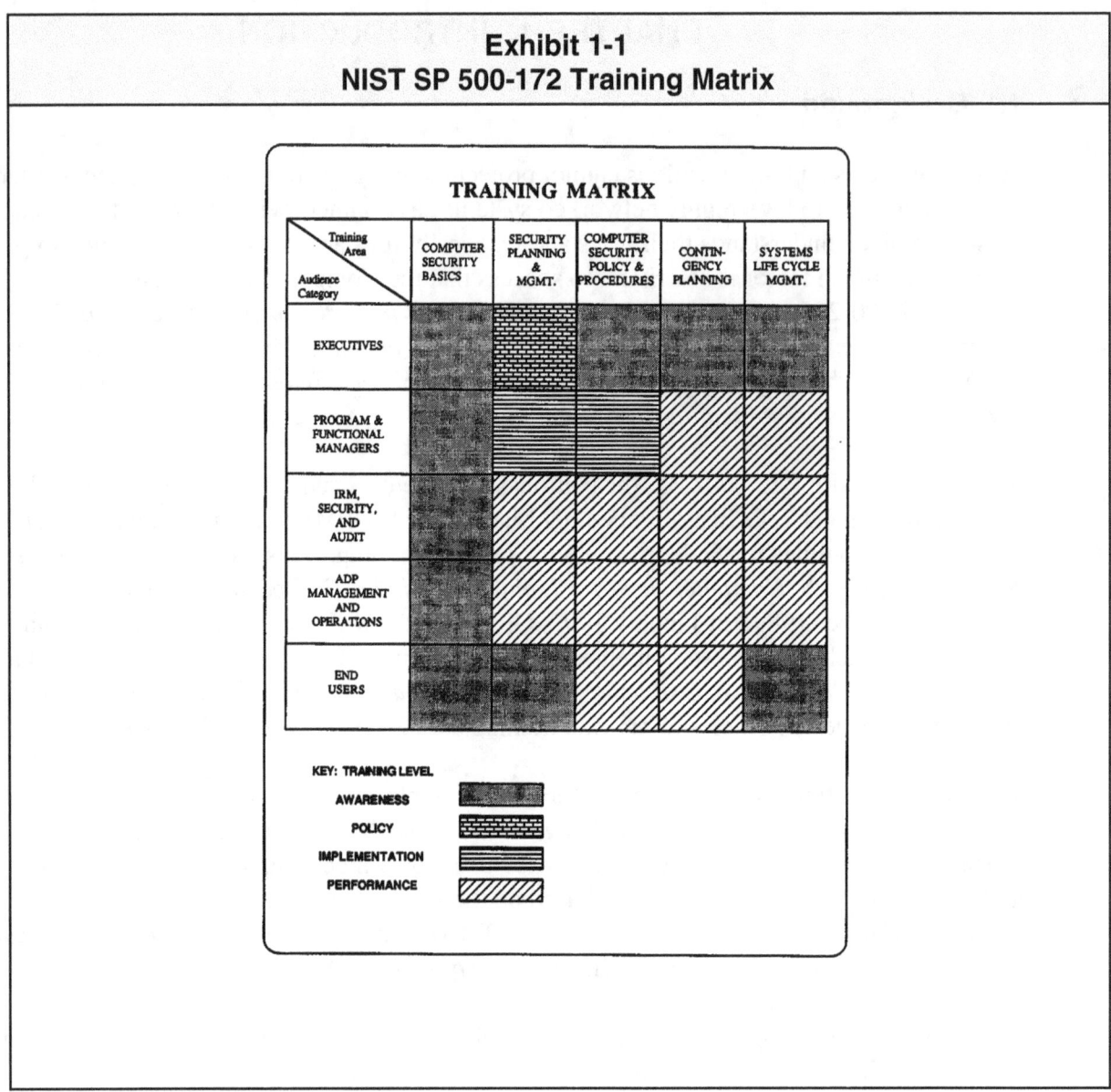

1.2 Purpose

OMB Circular A-130, as revised in 1996, required NIST to update SP 500-172. *As a result, this document supersedes SP 500-172 and presents a new conceptual framework for providing IT security training.* This framework includes the IT security training requirements appropriate for today's distributed computing environment and provides flexibility for extension to accommodate future technologies and the related risk management decisions.

1.3 Principles of the New Approach: Results-Based Learning

The learning approach presented in this document is designed on the following principles to facilitate results-based learning.

- **Focuses on job functions, or roles and responsibilities specific to individuals, not job titles, and recognizes that individuals have unique backgrounds, and therefore, different levels of understanding.**

    The earlier 500-172 focused on various categories of employees. This new approach recognizes that an individual may have more than one organizational role, and will need IT security training which satisfies the specific responsibilities of each role. In addition, because it is not focused on job titles, this approach facilitates more consistent interpretation of training criteria across organizations.

    Everyone needs basic training in IT security concepts and procedures. Beyond the basics, this new approach establishes three distinct levels of IT security training: Beginning, Intermediate, and Advanced. Each level is then linked to roles and responsibilities. Because individuals may perform more than one role within the organization, they may need intermediate or advanced level IT security training in their *primary* job role, but only the beginning level in a *secondary* or *tertiary* role. The new concept facilitates training tailored to individual employee needs and career mobility, and to an organization's evolving or changing mission and mix of job functions. Thus, the concept of refresher training (traditionally viewed as repetitive learning) gives way to the "just-in-time" learning approach, as an individual's or organization's IT security training needs evolve or change.

- **Delineates the differences among awareness, training, and education.**

    First, this approach considers *awareness* programs (which are generally well established in Federal agencies/organizations) as a pre-requisite to IT security *training*. This document defines the term "IT Security Basics and Literacy," as the transitional learning activity between "Awareness" and "Training." IT Security Basics and Literacy comprises relatively generic concepts, terms, and associated learning modules that do not significantly differ among categories of employees or organizations. Thus, this approach eliminates redundancies across audience categories and establishes a baseline of IT security knowledge across government which all employees can reasonably be expected to have as they change jobs and organizations. This *baseline* is independent of specific IT systems.

Second, the critical differences between "Training" and "Education" are often overlooked. "Education" is clearly identified in this new model as a separate learning level, while recognizing that the education level's applicability is limited to an organization's designated IT security specialists. Providing formal education to this group is outside the purview of most Federal agency training programs—with some notable exceptions among national security-related agencies. This document takes the view that education (as distinguished from training) and associated on-the-job experience are essential for IT security specialists to be able to fulfill their roles in an effective manner. The provision of specific criteria for the education level is beyond the scope of NIST's mandate and, therefore, is beyond the scope of this document.

- **Provides an integrated framework (planning tool) to identify training needs throughout the workforce and ensure that everyone receives appropriate training.**

    The model presented in this document relates job function to required IT security knowledge. This allows managers to identify the training needed to fulfill their IT security responsibilities, to understand the consequences of denying or deferring training, and to plan and schedule training according to organizational priorities.

- **Provides a course development tool.**

    Course developers can readily identify the learning outcomes expected for individuals in various roles with varying responsibilities. This will facilitate the development of IT security course material targeted to the needs of the Federal workforce and will encourage the development of "plug and play" training modules that can be readily customized or adapted to an organization's needs.

- **Provides a structure for evaluating learning effectiveness.**

    Providing training to individuals does not necessarily ensure that learning has occurred. Learning can best be demonstrated by subsequent on-the-job performance. This document's learning objectives are designed to be performance-based, rather than content-based, and to provide benchmarks for evaluating learning effectiveness. Further, this document requires evaluation as a component of an organization's IT security training program and provides an evaluation planning process and a discussion of levels of evaluation.

- **Is extensible.**

    This document is intended to be issued in looseleaf format for extensibility and ease of updating. It is designed to be used as a "living" handbook and reference, with evolving

Information Technology Security Training Requirements

criteria, exhibits, and appendices that will enable Federal agencies and organizations to ensure that their workforce keeps abreast of changes in information technology and the impact of such changes on the protection of information and systems.

1.4 Use of this Document

The overall goal for use of this document is to facilitate the development or strengthening of a comprehensive, measurable, cost-effective IT security program which supports the missions of the organization and is administered as an integral element of sound IT management and planning. Protecting the value of an organization's information assets demands no less. This approach allows senior officials to understand where, in what way, and to what extent IT-related job responsibilities include IT security responsibilities, permitting the most cost-effective allocation of limited IT security training resources.

The issuance of this document is not intended to significantly modify Federal agencies' ongoing IT security awareness programs and activities, or to invalidate their IT security training courses or courseware. Rather, their courses will require comprehensive review and revalidation in accordance with this new performance-based model and requirements. It is expected that agencies and organizations will find training gaps and will need to establish priorities and strategies for filling them. This process cannot be accomplished by a single organization's IT security program office working alone. Instead, it requires a broad, cross-organizational strategy at the executive level to bring together various functions and organization entities that may not have previously worked together. The perspectives and expertise of training center personnel, course designers, program analysts, IT security specialists, training evaluators, and specialists in many related IT functional areas all are needed to achieve success. To assist in achieving this goal, Exhibit 1-2, on the next page, identifies groups of individuals who will be able to use this guidance document and suggests ways in which they may want to use it.

1.5 Document Organization

This guidance document is organized as follows.

- **Chapter 1, Introduction:** Provides background information citing the statutory and regulatory requirements for IT security training. Establishes the purpose of this document in superseding NIST SP 500-172. Describes the principles of the role- and results-based approach to training taken in this document. Identifies who will be able to use this guidance and suggests ways of using the document.

Exhibit 1-2 Use of this Document	
Who Should Use This Document	**How This Document Can Be Used**
Management — all levels including team leaders, program managers, system managers, and organization leaders	• To determine staff training needs • To prioritize use of training resources • To evaluate training effectiveness
IT Security Specialists	• To identify training courses and training aids that meet established requirements • To identify training gaps and needs in the organization's IT security program • To determine the amount of course customization needed • To develop a compliance baseline for the organization
Training Professionals • Career Planners/Human Resource Personnel • Training Coordinators/Curriculum Developers • Course Developers • Trainers	• To gain an understanding of IT security requirements and the knowledges, skills, and abilities needed to meet those requirements • To evaluate course quality • To assist in obtaining appropriate courses and materials • To develop or customize courses/ materials • To tailor their teaching approach to achieve the desired behavioral outcomes
Every Employee	• To identify IT security training needs for their current job assignment and career path

- **Chapter 2, Learning Continuum — Model and Overview:** Introduces a role-based learning model that presents learning as a continuum from awareness through training to education and presents concepts associated with the model. Briefly discusses IT security awareness and education, and explains that detailed treatment of these areas is outside the scope of this document. Provides a comparison highlighting the differences among the three levels of learning and provides a transition to the following chapters, which concentrate on the two training layers of the model, Security Basics and Literacy and Roles and Responsibilities Relative to IT Systems. Discusses learning styles and effective teaching methods, ways of learning and implications for instruction, and presents some additional considerations for adult learning.

- **Chapter 3, IT Security Basics and Literacy:** Presents a core set of generic IT security terms and concepts for all Federal employees as a baseline for further, role-based learning, expands on those basic concepts, and provides a mechanism for students to relate and apply on the job the information learned.

- **Chapter 4, Training Development Methodology: Role-Based Training:** Builds on the Security Basics and Literacy training layer by presenting specific performance-based training requirements and outcomes mapped to job functions. Examines six role categories relative to IT systems—Manage, Acquire, Design and Develop, Implement and Operate, Review and Evaluate, and Use (with a seventh category, "Other" included to provide extensibility). Presents a matrix to relate the categories to three training content categories—Laws and Regulations, Security Program, and System Life Cycle Security. Identifies a set of 12 high-level IT security body of knowledge topics and concepts appropriate to each cell in the matrix from which curriculum content can be constructed. *The training requirements presented here were derived from the IT security program requirements established in Appendix III of OMB Circular A-130.*

- **Chapter 5, Evaluating Training Effectiveness:** Requires evaluation as a component of an organization's IT security training program. Identifies purposes of evaluation, presents progressive levels of training evaluation, and provides guidance in evaluation planning and implementation.

In addition, this document is supported by several Appendices designed to facilitate its ease of use and to amplify portions of the document which require a more in-depth treatment. These include the following.

- **Appendix A, Information Technology Security Learning Continuum:** Shows a full-page presentation of the Learning Model introduced in Chapter 2.

- **Appendix B, Information Technology Security Training Matrix:** Presents a full-page illustration of how the individual training modules fit together, as used in Chapter 4.

- **Appendix C, Glossary:** Defines key terms used in this document.

- **Appendix D, Selected Government IT Security References:** Provides documentation and sources of material which are related to Federal IT Security Training.

- **Appendix E, Job Function-Training Cross Reference:** Provides a graphical display of the training modules recommended for individuals performing a specific job function.

CHAPTER

2

LEARNING CONTINUUM - MODEL AND OVERVIEW

Information Technology Security Training Requirements

CHAPTER 2. LEARNING CONTINUUM — MODEL AND OVERVIEW

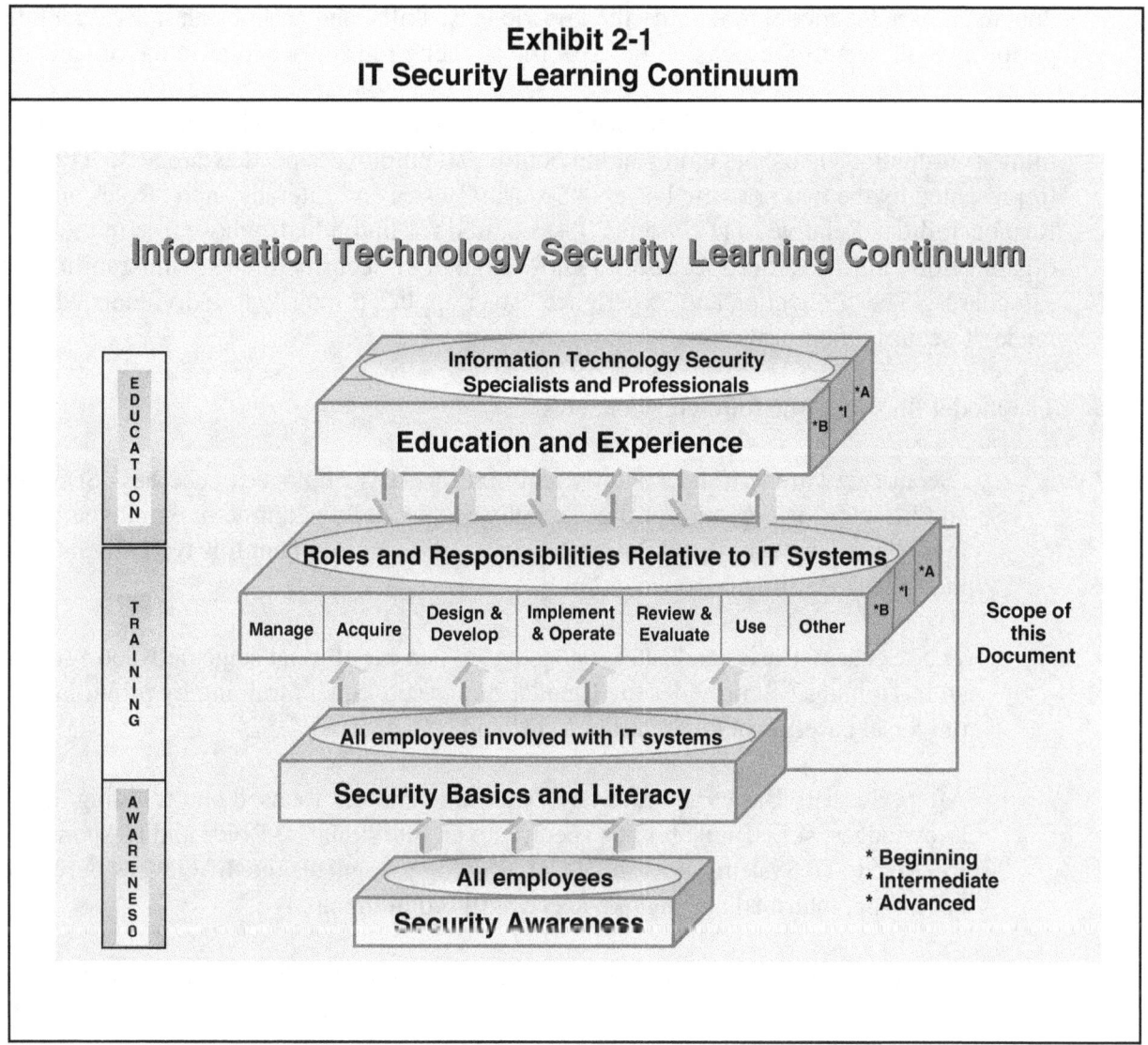

Exhibit 2-1
IT Security Learning Continuum

2.1 Introduction to the Model

The model presented as Exhibit 2-1 is based on the premise that learning is a continuum. Specifically, learning in this context starts with awareness, builds to training, and evolves into education. This model provides the context for understanding and using this document.

Information Technology Security Training Requirements

The model is role-based. It defines the IT security learning needed as a person assumes different roles within an organization and different responsibilities in relation to IT systems. This document uses the model to identify the knowledges, skills, and abilities an individual needs to perform the IT security responsibilities specific to each of his or her roles in the organization.

The type of learning that individuals need becomes more comprehensive and detailed at the top of the continuum. Thus, beginning at the bottom, all employees need awareness. Training (represented by the two bracketed layers "Security Basics and Literacy" and "Roles and Responsibilities Relative to IT Systems") is required for individuals whose role in the organization indicates a need for special knowledge of IT security threats, vulnerabilities, and safeguards. The "Education and Experience" layer applies primarily to individuals who have made IT security their profession.

The model illustrates the following concepts:

- "Security Awareness" is explicitly required for ALL employees, whereas "Security Basics and Literacy" is required for those employees, including contractor employees, who are involved in any way with IT systems. In today's environment this typically means all individuals within the organization.

- The "Security Basics and Literacy" category is a transitional stage between "Awareness" and "Training." It provides the foundation for subsequent training by providing a universal baseline of key security terms and concepts.

- After "Security Basics and Literacy," training becomes focused on providing the knowledges, skills, and abilities specific to an individual's "Roles and Responsibilities Relative to IT Systems." At this level, training recognizes the differences between beginning, intermediate, and advanced skill requirements.

- The "Education and Experience" level focuses on developing the ability and vision to perform complex multi-disciplinary activities and the skills needed to further the IT security profession and to keep pace with threat and technology changes.

Learning is a continuum in terms of levels of knowledge, but the acquisition or delivery of that knowledge need not proceed sequentially. Given resource constraints, organizations have a responsibility to evaluate against the continuum both the scope of their IT security training needs and the effectiveness of the training provided, to be able to allocate future training resources to derive the greatest value or return on investment.

Information Technology Security Training Requirements

2.2 Levels of Learning

2.2.1 Awareness

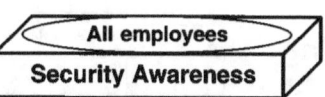

Awareness is not training. The purpose of awareness presentations is simply to focus attention on security. Awareness presentations are intended to allow individuals to recognize IT security concerns and respond accordingly. In awareness activities the learner is a recipient of information, whereas the learner in a training environment has a more active role. Awareness relies on reaching broad audiences with attractive packaging techniques. Training is more formal, having a goal of building knowledge and skills to facilitate job performance.

A few examples of IT security awareness materials/activities include:

- Promotional/speciality trinkets with motivational slogans,
- A security reminder banner on computer screens, which comes up when a user logs on,
- Security awareness video tapes, and
- Posters or flyers.

Effective IT security awareness presentations must be designed with the recognition that people tend to practice a tuning-out process called acclimation. If a stimulus, originally an attention-getter, is used repeatedly, the learner will selectively ignore the stimulus. Thus, awareness presentations must be on-going, creative, and motivational, with the objective of focusing the learner's attention so that the learning will be incorporated into conscious decision-making. This is called assimilation, a process whereby an individual incorporates new experiences into an existing behavior pattern.

Learning achieved through a single awareness activity tends to be short-term, immediate, and specific. Training takes longer and involves higher-level concepts and skills. For example, if a learning objective is "to facilitate the increased use of effective password protection among employees," an awareness activity might be the use of reminder stickers for computer keyboards. A training activity might involve computer-based instruction in the use of passwords, parameters, and how to change the passwords for organization systems.

Detailed guidance on IT security awareness is outside the scope of this document. Awareness, as originally defined in 1989 in NIST SP 500-172, "creates the [employee's] sensitivity to the threats and vulnerabilities of computer systems and the recognition of the need to protect data, information, and the means of processing them." The fundamental value of IT security awareness programs is that they set the stage for training by bringing about a change in attitudes which change the organizational culture. The cultural change is the realization that IT security is critical because a security failure has potentially adverse consequences for everyone. *Therefore, IT security is everyone's job.*

Chapter 2. Learning Continuum

Information Technology Security Training Requirements

2.2.2 Training
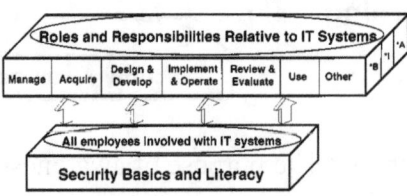

The "Training" level of the learning continuum strives to produce relevant and needed security skills and competency by practitioners of functional specialties other than IT security (e.g., management, systems design and development, acquisition, auditing). The training layers are discussed in detail in Chapters 3 (Security Basics and Literacy) and 4 (Training Development Methodology: Role-Based Training).

2.2.3 Education

The "Education" level integrates *all* of the security skills and competencies of the various functional specialties into a common body of knowledge, adds a multi-disciplinary study of concepts, issues, and principles (technological and social), and strives to produce IT security specialists and professionals capable of vision and pro-active response.

Historically, "computer security specialists" were practitioners appointed from the ranks of "computer specialists" (or another functional specialty), as if designation alone made those individuals specialists in security. Security responsibilities were often assigned as collateral to the duties of the primary functional specialty.

At best, Federal agencies paid for occasional training courses for their designated Computer Security Officers or specialists; but few agency officials recognized a need to enroll their designees in a formal computer security educational program—or required evidence of qualification or certification as a condition of appointment or collateral designation. IT Security professionalization was not mandated as a component of agency computer security training programs: it was outside the scope of the then-current Federal computer security training guidelines (SP 500-172).

Now, however, the IT Security Specialist/Officer/Program Manager functions have become too technologically and managerially complex to be successfully accomplished—especially on an ancillary or collateral basis—by practitioners lacking a comprehensive set of competencies. Moreover, organization officials, customers, technical personnel, and other stakeholders are creating pressures and demands for creative and dependable solutions to a growing range, number, and severity of security and privacy concerns—solutions which can only be achieved by a class of professionals with expertise in system and information protection. IT security professionalization is rapidly becoming a "business competency" in the public and private sectors.

IT security professionalization criteria are outside the scope of this document. The training guidance in Chapter 4 can be used and sequenced by agencies on an individualized basis as a cost-effective way to fill gaps in a given practitioner's knowledge and prepare him/her for formal education that may be needed for credentialing or other demonstrable measures of qualification in IT security.

An IT security professional is one who integrates the principles of the IT security field in a forward-looking manner to keep up with technology trends and their evolving security implications. At the "Training" level of the learning continuum, the specific knowledge and skills acquired may become obsolete as technology changes. The exploratory nature of education differentiates it from training. From this exploratory vantage point, advances in thought and theory make their way into security practices taught in training programs. The educated IT security professional has the comprehensive grasp of the field required to take responsibility for their further learning in an ever-changing environment.

At the advanced level of IT security professionalization, such as that of an IT Security Program Manager, an employee should be able to represent the organization and participate actively and constructively in addressing interagency or cross-cutting issues and concerns. Examples include increasing the effectiveness of assurance techniques; developing security policy models; participating in symposia or workgroups; or contributing to, developing, or managing training programs.

To reach the advanced level of IT security professionalization, completion of formal education in the field is required. With regard to formal education, organizational officials who appoint/supervise IT security specialists should know two important points: first, a concentration or major can be located in any of a number of departments or colleges—from business administration to computer science; and second, regardless of where a concentration or major may be placed in a given university, the program of study should incorporate a well-planned infusion of communications technology, human/behavioral science, mathematics, computer science, engineering, business ethics, and information law.

2.3 Comparative Framework

As illustrated in the learning continuum, "Awareness" constitutes the point-of-entry for all employees into the progression of IT security knowledge levels; the "Training" level, starting with "Security Basics and Literacy," then builds a wide range of security-related skills needed by employees in several functional area categories; and the "Education" level is the capstone of the learning continuum—creating expertise necessary for IT security specialists and professionals.

Thus, "In a training environment the employee is taught to use specific skills as part of exacting job performance. In an educational context the employee would be encouraged to examine and evaluate not only skills and methods of work but fundamental operating principles and tenets upon which job skills are based...."[1]

The distinction among the three levels is not always easy to interpret and apply. Exhibit 2-2, below, illustrates this distinction.

Exhibit 2-2 Comparative Framework[2]			
	AWARENESS	**TRAINING**	**EDUCATION**
Attribute:	"What"	"How"	"Why"
Level:	Information	Knowledge	Insight
Learning Objective:	Recognition and Retention	Skill	Understanding
Example Teaching Method:	Media - Videos - Newsletters - Posters	Practical Instruction - Lecture and/or demo - Case study - Hands-on practice	Theoretical Instruction - Seminar and discussion - Reading and study - Research
Test Measure:	True/False Multiple Choice (identify learning)	Problem Solving, i.e., Recognition and Resolution (apply learning)	Essay (interpret learning)
Impact Timeframe:	Short-term	Intermediate	Long-term

---

[1] "Computer Security Education, Training, and Awareness: Turning a Philosophical Orientation into Practical Reality," W.V. Maconachy, Proceedings of the 12th National Computer Security Conference, October 1988.

[2] "The Human Factor in Training Strategies," a presentation to the Federal Computer Security Program Managers' Forum, by Dorothea de Zafra, November, 1991.

2.4 Learning Styles and Effective Teaching Methods

Exhibit 2-2 illustrates learning objectives and examples of teaching methods at each level of the Learning Continuum. This section further develops the role and importance of teaching methods relative to learning for users of this document who may not be training professionals. The Federal workforce is the intended audience for this guidance document, and it is not a single, homogeneous entity. Therefore, no uniform teaching approach, or set of materials, is appropriate. Course developers and trainers will need to select the training materials and approaches that will best address the needs of given audiences in line with an organization's culture and requirements, as well as with individual student needs as outlined below.

2.4.1 Ways of Learning and Implications for Instruction

Individuals learn in different ways. The learning approach most effective for a particular individual is a function of their preferred learning style, education, and prior experience. While a discussion of learning theory is beyond the scope of this document, *it is important for subject matter specialists who may serve as instructors to know that students will not all take in and process information in the same way.* Attention to these differences in the instructional process is just as important as is attention to the subject matter itself.

> "I hear and I forget.
> I see and I remember.
> I do and I understand."
>
> — Chinese Proverb

Learning Style: Individuals learn in several ways but each person, as part of their personality, has a preferred or primary learning style. Instruction can positively or negatively affect a student's performance, depending on whether it is matched, or mismatched, with a student's preferred learning style. In learning *information or concepts*, some students will do better through reading (visual learning); others prefer to listen to a lecture (auditory learning); still others need to participate in a discussion (kinesthetic or tactile learning) in order to refine and finally grasp the material. In learning *practical skills*, some students prefer "how-to" pictures or diagrams (visual learning); others prefer to hear verbal instructions (auditory learning); still others ignore directions and prefer to jump in and figure things out as they go along (kinesthetic or tactile learning).

Content specialists tend to make the mistake of equating teaching to telling. They find out the hard way that students who do not learn best through listening will tune out lectures and learn little. Being aware of learning style differences should motivate instructors to use a variety of teaching approaches. For example, instructors who physically move around the classroom, who plan silent reading as well as lecturing, who include small group problem-solving, large group debate, brainstorming, blackboard diagraming and other visual aids will have something for everyone and in so doing will eliminate the "yawn factor." The implications for courseware developers is that there is substantial benefit in using flexible presentation formats (e.g., multimedia, searchable databases, text, graphics, simulations, team teaching, decision trees and interactive learning). A training program as a whole should ideally include a range of delivery approaches. These could include, in addition to classroom instruction and computer-based instruction, such options as manuals and self-paced instruction books, videotapes, interactive workshops with "hands-on" exercises, and one-on-one mentoring/coaching by senior staff.

Education and prior experience: Materials developers and trainers should consider the likely education and experience of their target audience and adjust their presentation approach and content accordingly. An individual with an advanced degree will perceive and learn new material in a manner that is different from an individual without a degree but who has extensive on-the-job experience. For example, individuals with more than 15 years of employment (e.g., an older audience) are less likely to be familiar with or comfortable with technology-oriented teaching techniques. However, if the target audience primarily consists of individuals who have recently graduated from college or high school (e.g., a younger audience), then increasing the proportion of material delivered through multimedia or computer-based instruction may be appropriate, as today's students are generally more experienced with these teaching approaches. The actual job functions of the target audience should also be considered when developing training materials and selecting teaching methodologies. For example, if instruction relating to the IT security countermeasures of a network server is being presented to an audience of system administrators, then a multi-day, hands-on approach might be most effective. If the same material is to be presented to a group of system designers, then a 2-hour lecture may be sufficient.

2.4.2 Additional Considerations for Adult Learning

Course developers and trainers should also be aware that adults have well established—not formative—values, beliefs, and opinions. Individuals have individual learning style preferences and adults may have had differing education, varying years of experience, and a wealth of previously learned information which they bring to the learning venue. Adults relate new information and knowledge to previously learned information, experiences, and values—sometimes consciously, sometimes unconsciously—thus, misperception and miscommunication can occur unless instructors make the effort to draw students out. This can be done (at least in a classroom setting) by balancing the presentation of new material with student sharing of relevant experiences. Instructors can help to make connections between various student opinions and ideas, while focusing class effort on integration of the new knowledge or skill with respect to its application.

Team teaching, if that is an option, can leverage individual instructor's respective skills in this regard. In any case, the involvement of adult students as resources can help overcome potential problems associated with classes composed of workforce students with differing levels of subject-matter knowledge. Otherwise, instructors who rely on giving a lecture of the material risk finding themselves over the heads of beginners, while boring or talking down to students who are at more advanced levels.

Finally, adult students, more so than their younger counterparts, learn best when they perceive the relevance of the knowledge or skill to their current job or to their career advancement. When the instructor is able to emphasize the applicability and practical purpose of the material to be mastered, as distinguished from abstract or conceptual learning, the learning retention rates and the subsequent transference of the new knowledge or skill to the students' jobs and organizational settings will be enhanced.

2.4.3 References

For further information, the following resources are suggested as a point of departure. This is not an exhaustive listing.

Cantor, Jeffrey A. Delivering Instruction to Adult Learners, Toronto: Wall & Emerson, 1992.

Hartman, Virginia R. "Teaching and learning style preferences: Transitions through technology." VCCA Journal, Vol.9, no. 2, pp. 18-20, 1995.

Kearsley, Greg. Andragogy (M. Knowles), Washington, DC: George Washington University, 1996.

Knowles, M.S. The Modern Practice of Adult Education: Andragogy vs. Pedagogy, New York: Association Press, 1970.

CHAPTER 3

SECURITY BASICS AND LITERACY

CHAPTER 3. SECURITY BASICS AND LITERACY

3.1 Definition and Purpose

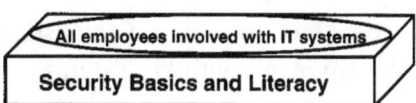

The Security Basics and Literacy level on the learning continuum is the transition between awareness and training. To draw an analogy with reading literacy, "awareness" is equivalent to reading readiness, whereby the child learns to recognize and memorize the letters of the alphabet. Then, at the transitional level, the child learns to use the alphabet and principles of grammar and sentence structure to read and become literate. The ability to read is the foundation for further, specific learning. So, too, are Security Basics and Literacy the foundation for further specific learning related to one's role(s) with respect to IT systems.

IT Security literacy must not be confused with the term "computer literacy," which refers to an individual's familiarity with a basic set of knowledge needed to use a computer. *IT Security literacy refers to an individual's familiarity with—and ability to apply—a core knowledge set (i.e., "IT security basics") needed to protect electronic information and systems.* Just as computer literacy is a generic foundation, i.e., is not geared to specific technology or application(s), so, too, is security literacy a one-size-fits-all foundation for further learning; it is not geared to any specific system. *All individuals who use computer technology or its output products, regardless of their specific job responsibilities, must know IT security basics and be able to apply them.*

The next step beyond IT Security Basics and Literacy is to focus individuals' ongoing learning on their respective job functions and the system(s) they are involved with. That focusing step or stage constitutes the beginning level of specific, role-based IT security *training*, and is covered in Chapter 4, Training Development Methodology: Role-Based Training. In Chapter 4, "beginning" refers to the beginning of IT security skills training, a logical segue from the knowledge base established here.

The Security Basics and Literacy level has the following learning objectives:

- To ensure that the student knows the "alphabet," i.e., a core set of key terms and essential concepts which comprises IT security and is essential for the protection of information and systems. (Many of the terms and concepts should have been previously introduced to the learner in an agency's awareness briefings or activities. In that case, Security Basics and Literacy properly provides reinforcement and structure.)

- To establish the principles for "reading" or "using the alphabet."

- To promote personal responsibility and positive behavioral change.

- To offer a curriculum framework to promote consistency across government.

These objectives are designed to permit a consistent, government-wide approach to ensure that all employees who are involved with IT systems—regardless of agency, organizational unit, job function(s), or specific system(s)—acquire the same, comprehensive literacy in security basics. The value of a consistent training program is the portability of security literacy as employees change jobs and organizations.

3.2 Basics — Core Set of IT Security Terms and Concepts

The body of knowledge associated with IT security is large and growing at an increasing rate, commensurate with today's rapid technological changes. Regardless of its size and growth rate, certain basic concepts form the foundation of any effective IT security program and environment. These terms and concepts must be learned ***and applied*** as the individual proceeds from security awareness to training and then to education.

The core set of IT security terms and concepts is presented in this section as the "ABC's of Information Technology Security," 26 items related to the alphabet, as summarized in Exhibit 3-1 on the next page and described briefly in Exhibit 3-2. This memory tool approach aids the learning process while communicating fundamental IT security concepts. It is anticipated that course material developed under this model will build on the memory tool approach to learning.

(Text continues after exhibits, on page 32.)

Exhibit 3-1
ABC's OF INFORMATION TECHNOLOGY SECURITY

A	**A**ssets - Something of value requiring protection (hardware, software, data, reputation)
B	**B**ackup - The three most important safeguards - backup, backup, backup
C	**C**ountermeasures and Controls - Prevent, detect, and recover from security incidents
D	**D**AA and Other Officials - Manage and accept risk and authorize the system to operate
E	**E**thics - The body of rules that governs an individual's behavior.
F	**F**irewalls and Separation of Duties - Minimize the potential for "incident encroachment"
G	**G**oals - Confidentiality, Integrity, and Availability (CIA)
H	**H**ackers/Crackers - Intruders who are threats to any system
I	**I**ndividual Accountability/Responsibility - Individuals responsible for their own actions
J	**J**ob Description/Job Function - Defines the individual's roles within the organization
K	**K**eys to Incident Prevention - Awareness, compliance, common sense
L	**L**aws and Regulations - Establish basic control/security objectives
M	**M**odel Framework - Relates training needs to roles and responsibilities
N	**N**eed to Know - Limits access to data, sets objective for ongoing learning
O	**O**wnership - Establishes responsibility/accountability for asset protection
P	**P**olicies and Procedures - What to accomplish and how to accomplish it
Q	**Q**uality Assurance/Quality Control - Ensure the integrity of the process
R	**R**isk Management - Balances potential adverse impact against safeguard cost
S	**S**ecurity Training - The best return on investment of any security safeguard
T	**T**hreats - Are always present, and generally occur when least expected
U	**U**nique Identifiers - Provide for individual accountability and facilitate access control
V	**V**ulnerabilities - Security weaknesses through which threats impact the system
W	**W**aste, Fraud, and Abuse - The three primary impacts of a security incident
X	e**X**pect the une**X**pected - Don't assume that because something hasn't happened, it won't
Y	**Y**ou - Your actions/inactions are critical to maintaining an effective security environment
Z	**Z**oning/Compartmentalization - Establish security layers and minimize incident impact

Exhibit 3-2
IT Security ABC's — Terms and Concepts

- **A**ssets — Assets are something of value that requires protection. The value of an asset may be monetary or non-monetary. For example, a computer system clearly has a monetary value that may be expressed in terms of its cost of acquisition or replacement. Data, however, is an asset that may have a monetary value (the cost to acquire), a non-monetary value (loss of public confidence regarding data accuracy), or both.

- **B**ackup — Backup for data and/or processes are critical safeguards in any IT security environment. The concept of backup includes creation and testing of disaster recovery and continuity of operations plans as well as preparation of copies of data files that are stored "out of harm's way."

- **C**ountermeasures and Controls — Countermeasures, controls, and safeguards are terms that are often used synonymously. They refer to the procedures and techniques used to prevent the occurrence of a security incident, detect when an incident is occurring or has occurred, and provide the capability to respond to or recover from a security incident. A safeguard may be a password for a user identifier, a backup plan that provides for offsite storage of copies of critical files, audit trails that allow association of specific actions to individuals, or any of a number of other technical or procedural techniques. Basically, a safeguard is intended to protect the assets and availability of IT systems.

- **D**AA and Other Officials — Individuals are responsible for allocating resources. Resources may be allocated to address IT security issues or any of a number of other competing organizational needs. The individual who has such authority for a specific IT system may be termed a Designated Accrediting Authority (DAA), Approving Authority, Authorizing Official, Recommending Official, or other titles specific to an organization. Whatever the title, the individual who has the authority to allocate resources is also responsible for balancing risks and costs and accepting any residual risks in making those decisions. The accrediting authorities are often helped in these decisions by certifying authorities who provide assessments of the technical adequacy of the current security environment and recommendations for resolving deficiencies or weaknesses.

- **E**thics — the body of rules that governs an individual's behavior. It is a product of that individual's life experiences and forms a basis for deciding what is right and wrong when making decisions. In today's environment, ethics are, unfortunately, situational (i.e., an individual's definition of what is right and wrong changes depending on the nature of a particular situation). For example, an individual may believe that it is wrong to break into someone's house, but does not think that it is wrong to break into someone's computer system.

Information Technology Security Training Requirements

Exhibit 3-2

IT Security ABC's — Terms and Concepts (Continued)

- **Firewalls and Separation of Duties** — Firewalls and separation of duties have similar structures and complementary objectives: a firewall is a technical safeguard that provides separation between activities, systems, or system components so that a security failure or weakness in one is contained and has no impact on other activities or systems (e.g., enforcing separation of the Internet from a Local Area Network). Separation of duties similarly provides separation, but its objective is to ensure that no single individual (acting alone) can compromise an application. In both cases, procedural and technical safeguards are used to enforce a basic security policy that high risk activities should be segregated from low risk activities and that one person should not be able to compromise a system.

- **Goals** — The goals of an IT security program can be summarized in three words: *confidentiality* - data must be protected against unauthorized disclosure; *integrity* - IT systems must not permit processes or data to be changed without authorization; and *availability* - authorized access to IT systems must be assured.

- **Hackers/Crackers** — The term "hacker" was originally coined to apply to individuals who focused on learning all they could about IT, often to the exclusion of many other facets of life (including sleeping and eating). A "cracker" is any individual who uses advanced knowledge of networks or the Internet to compromise network security. Typically, when the traditional hacker compromised the security of an IT system, the objective was academic (i.e., a learning exercise), and any resulting damage or destruction was unintentional. Currently, the term hacker is being more widely used to describe any individual who attempts to compromise the security of an IT system, especially those whose intention is to cause disruption or obtain unauthorized access to data. Hacker/cracker activity generally gets high press coverage even though more mundane security incidents caused by unintentional actions of authorized users tend to cause greater disruption and loss.

- **Individual Accountability/Responsibility** — A basic tenet of IT security is that individuals must be accountable for their actions. If this is not followed and enforced, it is not possible to successfully prosecute those who intentionally damage or disrupt systems, or to train those whose actions have unintended adverse effects. The concept of individual accountability drives the need for many security safeguards such as user identifiers, audit trails, and access authorization rules.

- **Job Description/Job Function** — To provide individuals with the training necessary to do their job, and to establish appropriate safeguards to enforce individual accountability, it is necessary to know what functions an individual is authorized to perform (i.e., their role(s) within the organization). Some times this is accomplished using formalized/written job descriptions. In other situations, such assessments are based on analysis of the functions performed.

Chapter 3. Security Basics and Literacy

Exhibit 3-2
IT Security ABC's — Terms and Concepts (Continued)

- **K**eys to Incident Prevention — Many IT security incidents are preventable if individuals incorporate three basic concepts into their day-to-day activities: one, awareness - individuals should be aware of the value of the assets they use to do their job and the nature of associated threats and vulnerabilities; two, compliance - individuals should comply with established safeguards (e.g., scanning diskettes, changing passwords, performing backups); and three, common sense - if something appears too good to be true, it generally is.

- **L**aws and Regulations — Congress has enacted a number of laws (e.g., Privacy Act, Computer Security Act, Computer Fraud and Abuse Act) that establish the basic policy structure for IT security in the Federal government. These laws have been augmented with regulations and guidance regarding their applicability to IT systems. Private industry generally grounds its security policies on the impact on profitability and potential risk of lawsuits, as there are few specific legal requirements. The commonality between Federal and private IT security programs demonstrates that the objectives are the same whether the impetus was a law or the bottom line.

- **M**odel Framework — This document presents a model framework for IT security training. The model framework describes individual training needs relative to job function or role within the organization. The model recognizes that an individual's need for IT security training will change, both in scope and depth, relative to their organizational responsibilities.

- **N**eed to Know — Need to Know is addressed from two perspectives: first, a need for access to information to do a job; and second, need to know as a driver for continued learning. In the first case, access to information and processes should be restricted to that which the individual requires to do their job. This approach minimizes the potential for unauthorized activities, and maximizes the potential that the individual knows and understands the nature of the threats and vulnerabilities associated with their use or maintenance of an IT system; and second, given the rate of technological change, individuals need to know the characteristics of those technologies so they may be better able to address specific vulnerabilities.

- **O**wnership — Responsibility for the security of an IT system or asset must be assigned to a single, identifiable entity, and to a single, senior official within that entity. This provides for accountability for security failures and establishment of the chain of command that authorizes access to and use of system assets. This concept of individual responsibility and authority is generally termed ownership or stewardship. The ownership of an asset (particularly data) is generally retained, even when that asset is transferred to another organization. For example, tax data shared with other Federal and state agencies by the Internal Revenue Service must be secured in accordance with the Internal Revenue Code.

Exhibit 3-2
IT Security ABC's — Terms and Concepts   (Continued)

- **P**olicies and **P**rocedures — IT security safeguards are intended to achieve specific control objectives. These objectives are contained within security policies that should be tailored to the needs of each IT system. Procedures define the technical and procedural safeguards that have been implemented to enforce the specified policies. IT security procedures may be documented in a security plan.

- **Q**uality Assurance/**Q**uality Control — Quality Assurance and Quality Control are two processes that are used to ensure the consistency and integrity of security safeguards. Specifically, these processes are intended to ensure that security countermeasures perform as specified, under all workload and operating conditions.

- **R**isk Management — Risk management is the process whereby the threats, vulnerabilities, and potential impacts from security incidents are evaluated against the cost of safeguard implementation. The objective of Risk Management is to ensure that all IT assets are afforded reasonable protection against waste, fraud, abuse, and disruption of operations. Risk Management is growing in importance as the scope of potential threats is growing while available resources are declining.

- **S**ecurity Training — Security training is the sum of the processes used to impart the body of knowledge associated with IT security to those who use, maintain, develop, or manage IT systems. A well trained staff can often compensate for weak technical and procedural safeguards. Security training has been demonstrated to have the greatest return on investment of any technical or procedural IT security safeguard.

- **T**hreats — Threats are actions or events (intentional or unintentional) which, if realized, will result in waste, fraud, abuse, or disruption of operations. Threats are always present, and the rate of threat occurrence can not be controlled. IT security safeguards, therefore, must be designed to prevent or minimize any impact on the affected IT system.

- **U**nique Identifiers — A unique identifier is a code or set of codes that provide a positive association between authorities and actions to individuals. Safeguards must be in place to ensure that an identifier is used only by the individual to whom it is assigned.

- **V**ulnerabilities — Vulnerabilities are weaknesses in an IT system's security environment. Threats may exploit or act through a vulnerability to adversely affect the IT system. Safeguards are used to mitigate or eliminate vulnerabilities.

- **W**aste, Fraud, and Abuse — Waste, fraud, and abuse are potential adverse impacts that may result from a breakdown in IT security. Waste, fraud, and abuse are specifically identified as potential impacts in government-wide policy.

Exhibit 3-2

IT Security ABC's — Terms and Concepts (Continued)

- e**X**pect the une**X**pected — IT security safeguards target unauthorized actions. Unauthorized actions (acts by individuals or Acts-of-God) can take many forms and can occur at any time. Thus, security safeguards should be sufficiently flexible to identify and respond to any activity that deviates from a pre-defined set of acceptable actions.

- **Y**ou — You are responsible and will be held accountable for your actions relative to an IT system or its associated data. You can strengthen or weaken an IT security environment by your actions or inactions. For example, you can strengthen an IT environment by changing passwords at appropriate intervals and weaken it by failing to do so.

- **Z**oning/Compartmenting — Zoning/Compartmenting is a concept whereby an application is segmented into independent security environments. A breach of security would require a security failure in two or more zones/compartments before the application is compromised. This layered approach to security can be applied within physical or technical environments associated with an IT system.

3.3 Literacy — Curriculum Framework

The literacy level is the first solid step of the IT security training level, where the knowledge obtained through training can be directly related to the individual's role in his or her specific organization. Although the curriculum framework, presented below, provides a generic outline for material to be included in literacy training throughout government, it is imperative that the instructor relate the actual course content to the organization's unique culture and mission requirements. Emphasis placed on the specific topics may vary by student audience or organization needs. The curriculum framework was developed to present topics and concepts in a logical order, based on IT system planning and life cycle stages, but may be presented in any order. Literacy training may also be divided into more than one session. Regardless of the training method or structure used, it is expected that the actual literacy training, including all topics and concepts in the curriculum framework, can be completed within an 8-hour time frame. This is because, at the literacy level, the material should be presented as an introduction of the concepts and topics only.

There are a variety of suitable approaches for teaching this subject matter. One of the most effective is to encourage participation by the students in interactive discussions on how the various concepts relate to their particular organization or roles. This approach allows the students to understand the significance of IT security principles and procedures to their organization, and to begin finding ways of applying this new knowledge in their work environment.

Information Technology Security Training Requirements

The following curriculum framework incorporates and expands on the basic concepts introduced in the ABC's, introduces a set of generic topics and concepts which have been identified as the foundation for IT security training, and provides a mechanism for students to relate and apply the information learned on the job. In Chapter 4, a methodology for development of role-based training, based on an expanded version of these same (generic) topics and concepts, is presented to provide for the in-depth training requirements of individuals who have been assigned specific IT security related responsibilities.

1. **Laws and Regulations**

   Subjects to include:

   - Federal IT security laws, regulations, standards and guidelines
   - Organization specific policies and procedures
   - Role of Federal government-wide and organization specific laws, regulations, policies, guidelines, standards and procedures in protecting the organization's IT resources
     - Tangible and intangible IT resources (assets)
   - Current and emerging social issues that can affect IT assets
   - Laws and regulations related to social issues affecting security issues
   - Effect of social issues on accomplishment of organizations mission(s)
     - Social conflicts with the Freedom of Information Act
     - Public concern for protection of personal information
   - Legal and liability issues
     - Laws concerning copyrighted software
     - Organization policies concerning copyrighted software
     - Laws concerning privacy of personal information
     - Organization policies concerning privacy of personal information
     - Mission related laws and regulations
     - Effects of laws, regulations or policies on the selection of security controls

   Includes basic IT security concepts introduced in the following ABC's:

   L - Laws and Regulations
   P - Policies and Procedures

2. **The Organization and IT Security**

   Subjects to include:

   - Organization mission(s)
   - How information technology supports the mission(s)
   - Reliance on IT systems for mission accomplishment
   - IT security programs protect against violations of laws and regulations
   - Purpose and elements of organizational IT security programs

Chapter 3. Security Basics and Literacy

- Difference between organization level and system level IT security programs
- Changing IT security issues and requirements
- System ownership and its importance from a user or client perspective
- Information ownership and its importance from a user or client perspective
- Identification of IT security program and system level points of contacts

Includes basic IT security concepts introduced in the following ABC's:

    A - Assets
    G - Goals
    O - Ownership

3. **System Interconnection and Information Sharing**

   Subjects to include:

   - Increased vulnerabilities of interconnected systems and shared data
   - Responsibilities of system or information owner organizations if systems have external users or clients
   - Responsibility of users or clients for notifying system owners of security requirements
   - Sharing information on system controls with internal and external users and clients
   - Formal agreements between systems for mutual protection of shared data and resources
     - User rules of behavior and individual accountability in interconnected systems
     - System rules of behavior and technical controls based on most stringent protection requirements
   - Electronic mail security concerns
   - Electronic commerce
     - Electronic Fund Transfer
     - Electronic Data Interchange
     - Digital/electronic signatures
   - Monitoring user activities

   Includes basic IT security concepts introduced in the following ABC's:

       A - Assets
       C - Countermeasures and Controls
       E - Ethics
       H - Hackers/Crackers
       I - Individual Accountability/Responsibility
       T - Threats
       V - Vulnerabilities
       W - Waste, Fraud, and Abuse
       X - eXpect the uneXpected
       Y - You

Information Technology Security Training Requirements

4. **Sensitivity**

   Subjects to include:

   - Categorization of system sensitivity
     - Criticality
     - Unauthorized use
     - Reliability
   - Categorization of information sensitivity
     - Sensitive information in general
       - Types of sensitive information
       - Aggregation of information
     - Organization's sensitive information
       - Need to know
       - Authorized access
       - Unauthorized disclosure
   - IT asset protection requirements
   - The organization's need for confidentiality of its information
     - Adverse consequences of unauthorized information disclosure
   - The organization's need for integrity of its information
     - Corruption of information
       - Accidental
       - Intentional
     - Adverse consequences if public or other users do not trust integrity and reliability of information
   - The organization's need for availability of its information and IT systems
     - Adverse consequences of system or information unavailability
     - Public dependance on information
     - Internal or external user's dependence on information

   Includes basic IT security concepts introduced in the following ABC's:

   G - Goals
   N - Need to Know

5. **Risk Management**

   Subjects to include:

   - Managing risk
     - Threats
     - Vulnerabilities
     - Risk

Chapter 3. Security Basics and Literacy

Information Technology Security Training Requirements

- • Relationships between threats, vulnerabilities, risks
- Threats from "authorized system users"
- Increased threats and vulnerabilities from connection to external systems and networks
  - • "Hacker" threats
  - • Malicious software programs and virus threats
- Types of security controls (safeguards, countermeasures)
  - • Management controls
  - • Acquisition/development/installation/implementation controls
  - • Operational controls
  - • Security awareness and training controls
  - • Technical controls
- How different categories of controls work together
- Examples of security controls for:
  - • Confidentiality protection
  - • Availability protection
  - • Integrity protection
- Added security controls for connecting external systems and networks
- Protecting assets through IT security awareness and training programs
- Contingency-disaster recovery planning
  - • Importance of plan to deal with unexpected problems
  - • Importance of testing plan and applying lessons learned
- "Acceptable levels of risk" vs. "absolute protection from risk"
- "Adequate" and "appropriate" controls
  - • Unique protection requirements of IT systems and information
  - • Severity, probability, and extent of potential harm
  - • Cost effective/cost benefits
  - • Reduction of risk vs. elimination of risk
- Working together with other security disciplines
- Importance of internal and external audits, reviews, and evaluations in security decisions

Includes basic IT security concepts introduced in the following ABC's:

    C - Countermeasures and Controls
    R - Risk Management
    S - Security Training

6. Management Controls

Subjects to include:

- System/application-specific policies and procedures
- Standard operating procedures

Chapter 3. Security Basics and Literacy

- Personnel security
  - Background investigations/security clearances
  - Roles and responsibilities
  - Separation of duties
  - Role-based access controls
- System rules of behavior contribute to an effective security environment
  - Organization-specific user rules
  - System-specific user rules
    - Assignment and limitation of system privileges
    - Intellectual property/Copyright issues
    - Remote access and work at home issues
    - Official vs. unofficial system use
    - individual accountability
    - Sanctions or penalties for violations
- Individual accountability contributes to system and information quality
  - Individual acceptance of responsibilities
  - Signed individual accountability agreements
- IT security awareness and training
  - Determining IT security training requirements for individuals
  - Effect of IT security awareness and training programs on personal responsibility and positive behavioral changes
  - "Computer ethics"
  - System-specific user IT security training
- User responsibilities for inappropriate actions of others

Includes basic IT security concepts introduced in the following ABC's:

E - Ethics
I - Individual Accountability/Responsibility
J - Job Description/Job Function
M - Model Framework
P - Policies and Procedures
S - Security Training
Y - You

7. Acquisition/Development/Installation/Implementation Controls

Subjects to include:

- System life cycle stages and functions
- IT security requirements in system life cycle stages
  - Initiation stage
  - Development stage

- Test and evaluation stage
- Implementation stage
- Operations stage
- Termination stage
- Formal system security plan for management of a system
  - Identification of system mission, purpose and assets
  - Definition of system protection needs
  - Identification of responsible people
  - Identification of system security controls in-place or planned and milestone dates for implementation of planned controls
- Relationship of configuration and change management programs to IT security goals
- Testing system security controls synergistically and certification
- Senior manager approval (accredit) an IT system for operation

Includes basic IT security concepts introduced in the following ABC's:

D - DAA and Other Officials
G - Goals
O - Ownership

8. Operational Controls

Subjects to include:

- Physical and environmental protection
  - Physical access controls
  - Intrusion detection
  - Fire/water/moisture/heat/electrical maintenance
  - Mobile and portable systems
- Marking, handling, shipping, storing, cleaning, and clearing
- Contingency planning
  - Importance of developing and testing contingency/disaster recovery plans
  - Importance of users providing accurate information about processing needs, allowable down time and applications that can wait
  - Responsibility for backup copies of data files and software programs
  - Simple user contingency planning steps

Includes basic IT security concepts introduced in the following ABC's:

B - Backup
Z - Zoning/Compartmentalization

Information Technology Security Training Requirements

9. **Technical Controls**

   Subjects to include:

   - How technical (role-based access) controls support management (security rules) controls
     - User identification and passwords/tokens
     - User role-based access privileges
     - Public access controls
   - How system controls can allow positive association of actions to individuals
     - Audit trails
     - System monitoring
   - Recognizing attacks by hackers, authorized or unauthorized users
     - Effects of hacker attack on authorized users
     - Unauthorized use or actions by authorized users
     - Reporting incidents
   - User actions to prevent damage from malicious software or computer virus attacks
     - Organization specific procedures for reporting virus incidents
     - Technical support and help from security incident response teams
     - Software products to scan, detect and remove computer viruses
   - Role of cryptography in protecting information

   Includes basic IT security concepts introduced in the following ABC's:

   F - Firewalls and Separation of Duties
   H - Hackers/Crackers
   I - Individual Accountability/Responsibility
   J - Job Description/Job Function
   K - Keys to Incident Prevention
   Q - Quality Assurance/Quality Control
   U - Unique Identifiers
   V - Vulnerabilities
   Z - Zoning/Compartmentalization

CHAPTER 4

TRAINING DEVELOPMENT METHODOLOGY: ROLE-BASED TRAINING

Information Technology Security Training Requirements

CHAPTER 4. TRAINING DEVELOPMENT METHODOLOGY: ROLE-BASED TRAINING

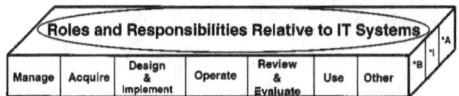

4.1 Introduction

The Learning Continuum presented in Chapter 2 shows the relationship among Awareness, Security Basics and Literacy, Training, and Education. The Continuum demonstrates that Awareness and Security Basics and Literacy form the baseline which is required for all individuals involved with the management, development, maintenance, and/or use of IT systems. It also demonstrates that Training and Education are to be provided selectively, based on individual responsibilities and needs. Specifically, Training is to be provided to individuals based on their particular job functions. Education is intended for designated IT security specialists in addition to role-based training. This chapter establishes a model and requirements for the Roles and Responsibilities Relative to IT Systems layer of the Learning Continuum.

Over time, individuals acquire different roles relative to the use of IT within an organization, or as they make a career move to a different organization. Sometimes they will be users of applications; in other instances they may be involved in developing a new system; and in some situations they may serve on a source selection board to evaluate vendor proposals for IT systems. An individual's need for IT security training changes as their roles change. This is recognized within the Learning Continuum by segmenting the Training level shown above into six functional specialities which represent categories of generic organizational roles: Manage, Acquire, Design and Develop, Implement and Operate, Review and Evaluate, and Use. A seventh category, "Other," is a place holder, to allow the matrix to be updated to accommodate any additional functional roles identified in the future.

This chapter examines the six role categories relative to three fundamental training content categories:

- Laws and Regulations—the types of knowledge, skills, and abilities (KSAs) relative to the laws and regulations pertaining to information and asset protection that govern the management and use of IT within the Federal Government. These include government-wide requirements such as the Computer Security Act of 1987, policy promulgated by the Office of Management and Budget, standards and guidance disseminated by NIST, as well as policies and procedures specific to a Department or agency;

- Security Program— KSAs relative to the establishment, implementation, and monitoring of an IT Security Program within an organization; and

Chapter 4. Training Development Methodology

Information Technology Security Training Requirements

- System Life Cycle Security— KSAs relative to the nature of IT security needed throughout each phase of a given system's life cycle. In this instance, a six-phased system life cycle model was used (Initiation, Development, Test and Evaluation, Implementation, Operations, and Termination).

Combining the six role categories and the three training areas (with a fourth area, "Other," added as a place holder for future use) yields the following Information Technology Security Training Matrix, Exhibit 4-1, shown below. This matrix is, in effect, a "pull-down menu" of the Training level in the Learning Continuum.

Exhibit 4-1
IT Security Training Matrix

	TRAINING AREAS	FUNCTIONAL SPECIALTIES						
		A MANAGE	B ACQUIRE	C DESIGN & DEVELOP	D IMPLEMENT & OPERATE	E REVIEW & EVALUATE	F USE	G OTHER
1	LAWS & REGULATIONS	1A	1B	1C	1D	1E	1F	▓
2	SECURITY PROGRAM							
2.1	PLANNING	2.1A	2.1B	2.1C	2.1D	2.1E	▓	▓
2.2	MANAGEMENT	2.2A	2.2B	2.2C	2.2D	2.2E	▓	▓
3	SYSTEM LIFE CYCLE SECURITY							
3.1	INITIATION	3.1A	3.1B	3.1C	▓	3.1E	3.1F	▓
3.2	DEVELOPMENT	3.2A	3.2B	3.2C	3.2D	3.2E	3.2F	▓
3.3	TEST & EVALUATION	▓	▓	3.3C	3.3D	3.3E	3.3F	▓
3.4	IMPLEMENTATION	3.4A	3.4B	3.4C	3.4D	3.4E	3.4F	▓
3.5	OPERATIONS	3.5A	3.5B	3.5C	3.5D	3.5E	3.5F	▓
3.6	TERMINATION	3.6A	▓	▓	3.6D	3.6E	▓	▓
4	OTHER	▓	▓	▓	▓	▓	▓	▓

This chapter presents the training requirements for each of the 46 cells, i.e., 1A through 3.6E. (Bricked cells - particularly 3.1D, 3.3A, 3.3B, 3.6B, and 3.6C - are place holders, or cells that may be used later.) This approach will enable course developers to create a block or module of instructional material relative to the requirements defined in a specific cell with confidence that it will complement and augment training material developed for the other cells. Further, individuals or supervisors will be able to select that training needed to satisfy an individual's organizational role at a specific point in time, with assurance that such training will contribute to his or her career progression, or to other assigned duties. Finally, trainers will have the flexibility to combine modules (horizontally or vertically) into a comprehensive IT security course or to insert one or more of the security modules into a training course for one of the functional specialties, such as management, acquisitions, or auditing.

Each cell of the IT Security Training Matrix is detailed in a one-page table, which has the format of the table shown in Exhibit 4-2. Explanation of the cell contents follows:

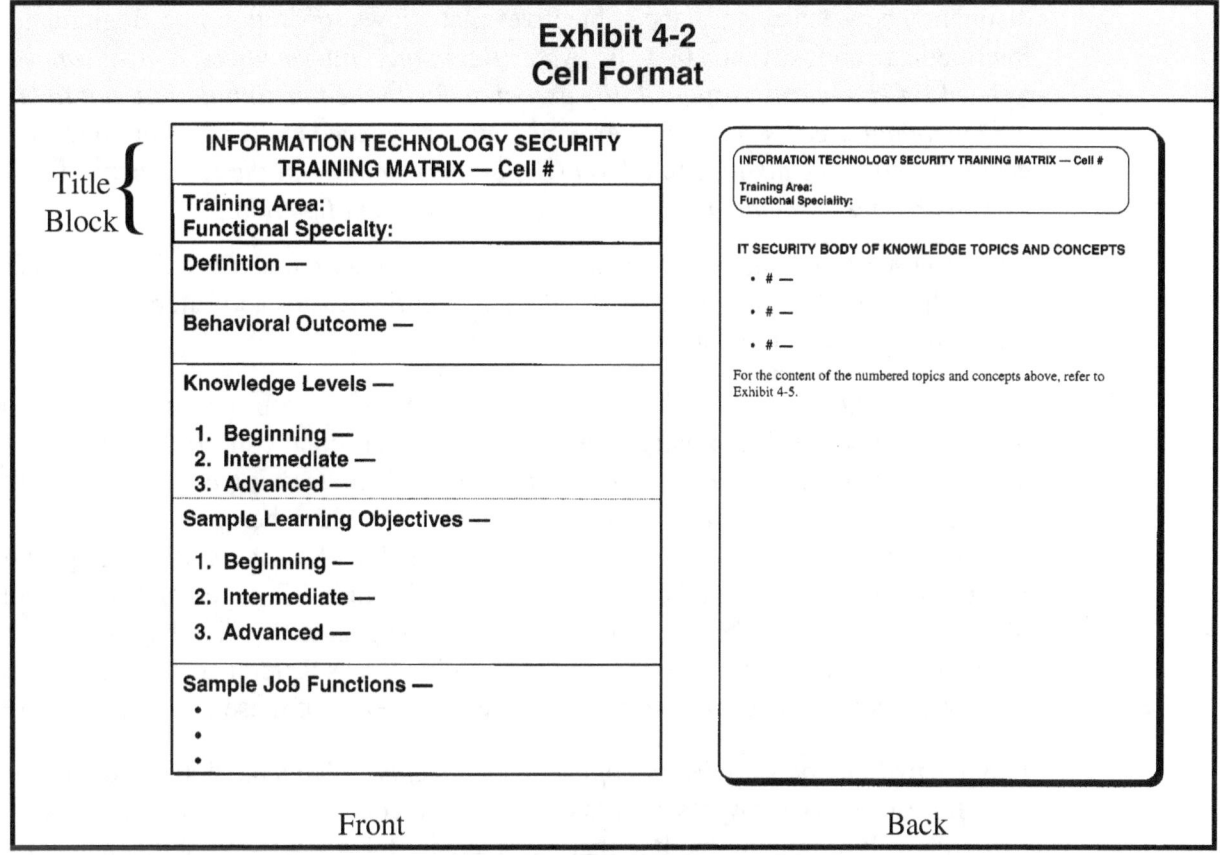

- *Title Block* — Labels the cell within the matrix and identifies the specific Training Area and Functional Specialty (Role) addressed.

- *Definition* — Defines the training content area addressed.

- *Behavioral Outcome* — Describes what an individual who has completed the specific training module is expected to be able to accomplish in terms of IT security-related job performance.

- *Knowledge Levels* — Provides verbs that describe actions an individual should be capable of performing on the job after completion of the training associated with the cell. The verbs are identified for three training levels: Beginning, Intermediate, and Advanced.

- *Sample Learning Objectives* — Links the verbs from the "Knowledge Levels" section to the "Behavioral Outcomes" by providing examples of the activities an individual should be capable of doing after successful completion of training associated with the cell. Again, the Learning Objectives recognize that training must be provided at Beginning, Intermediate, and Advanced levels. For some of the cells, there will not be three distinct levels (i.e., there may be only two levels or even one). In these instances, there is no clear distinction between performance objectives that allows separation into Beginning, Intermediate, and Advanced levels. *(Note: Beginning, Intermediate, and Advanced refer to levels of IT security responsibility associated with the functional area, not to levels of the functional area as such. For example, an experienced (Advanced level) IT system developer could be taking entry-level (Beginning) training in the IT security responsibilities associated with the system development function.)*

  The purpose of the Beginning Level is to focus the generic understanding of IT security, which the individual will have acquired from Security Basics and Literacy (per Chapter 3), on their job requirements.

- *Sample Job Functions* — Presents sample position titles or job functions of individuals who would be expected to obtain the training for a particular cell. *Individuals designated as IT Security specialists need to be acquainted with the training content in all cells, whether or not they themselves need training in a specific programmatic role (e.g., responsibility for selecting a back-up site for a specific IT system).* An aggregate of 26 Sample Job Functions for all cells is presented as Exhibit 4-3, together with the number of cells in which each occurs. It is not intended to be an exhaustive list of all possible job functions. Appendix E, Job Function-Training Cross Reference, contains tables that show the recommended training modules (cells) for each of these 26 job functions.

- *IT Security Body of Knowledge Topics and Concepts* — This block (on the back of the page for each cell), provides suggested topics and concepts which pertain to the particular cell or training module that will increase the knowledge, skills, and abilities of the student. The numbers on the back of the cell page refer to Exhibit 4-4, which presents twelve high-level topics and concepts intended to incorporate the overall body of knowledge required for training in IT security. Each of these topics and concepts is then broken down into more specific subjects that should be included in the training for that topic. By identifying the twelve topics and concepts at a high level, they become general and flexible categories under which more specific topics or subjects can be added or removed to keep up with evolving technology, laws, regulations, policies, or guidance.

  To customize the training in a cell, topics and detailed subjects may be presented at different depths to accomplish the desired learning objective level (i.e., Beginning, Intermediate, and Advanced). For example, if an individual has no acquisition responsibilities and therefore, no need for in-depth training in acquisition, that topic might be introduced, but not explained in depth. Thus, the student would become familiar with the associated IT security considerations, but would not learn how to write detailed IT security requirements for a statement of work. In addition, the content may be modified for specific organization or system reasons. *The listed topics and concepts are not intended to be absolute, and creators of the actual training courses will be expected to review the suggested topics for each cell and revise them as appropriate.*

No. of Cells	Exhibit 4-3 Frequency of Sample Job Function Occurrence
46	IT Security Officer/Manager*
18	System Owner
16	Information Resources Manager
15	Program Manager
11	Auditor, Internal
10	Network Administrator
10	System Administrator
10	System Designer/Developer
9	Auditor, External
8	Contracting Officer's Technical Representative (COTR)
8	Programmer/Systems Analyst
8	Systems Operations Personnel
8	Information Resources Management Official, Senior
7	Chief Information Officer
7	Database Administrator
7	Data Center Manager
6	Certification Reviewer
6	Contracting Officer
6	User
5	Designated Approving Authority (DAA)
5	Technical Support Personnel
3	Records Management Official
3	Source Selection Board Member
2	Freedom of Information Act Official
2	Privacy Act Official
2	Telecommunications Specialist

* Includes Information System Security Officer (ISSO), Network Security Officer (NSO), AIS Computer Security Officer (ACSO), Computer Security Officer (CSO), and other similar titles agencies may designate.

Exhibit 4-4
IT Security Body of Knowledge Topics and Concepts

This exhibit presents a comprehensive body of knowledge, topics, and concepts in the IT security field. It was developed by comparing, categorizing and combining the topics, concepts, and subjects from the following sources: OMB Circular A-130, Appendix III, *"Security of Federal Automated Information Resources;"* OMB Bulletin 90-08 (revised, currently in draft as *"User Guide for Developing and Evaluating Security Plans for Unclassified Federal Automated Information Systems");* NIST SP 800-12, *"An Introduction to Computer Security: The NIST Handbook;"* NIST SP 800-14, *"Generally Accepted Principles and Practices for Securing Information Technology Systems;"* and the unpublished Body of Knowledge material developed over a 2-year period (1993-1995) by a group of more than 150 IT security professionals from industry and a wide spectrum of Federal Government agencies.

1. LAWS AND REGULATIONS

    Federal government-wide and organization-specific laws, regulations, policies, guidelines, standards, and procedures mandating requirements for the management and protection of information technology resources.

    Federal Laws and Regulations
    Federal Standards and Guidelines
    Legal and Liability Issues
    Organization Policy, Guidelines, Standards and Procedures Development
    Organization Program
    Issue-specific
    System-specific

2. IT SECURITY PROGRAM

    A program established, implemented, and maintained to assure that adequate IT security is provided for all organizational information collected, processed, transmitted, stored, or disseminated in its general support systems and major applications.

    Organization-wide IT Security Program
    System-level IT Security Program
    Elements of IT Security Program
    Roles, Responsibilities, and Accountability
        Senior Management
        Organization-wide IT Security Managers
        Program and Functional Managers
        System/Application Owners
        Information Owner/Custodian
        IT System Security Managers
        Contractors
        Related Security Program Managers
        Users

Exhibit 4-4 (Continued)
IT Security Body of Knowledge Topics and Concepts

3. SYSTEM ENVIRONMENT

   The unique technical and operating characteristics of an IT system and its associated environment, including the hardware, software, firmware, communications capability, and physical location.

   IT Architecture
   Hardware Types
   Operating Software
   Application Software
   Communication Requirements
   Facilities Planning
   Processing Workflow
   Utility Software
   Associated Threats
   Associated Vulnerabilities

4. SYSTEM INTERCONNECTION

   The requirements for communication or interconnection by an IT system with one or more other IT systems or networks, to share processing capability or pass data and information in support of multi-organizational or public programs.

   Communications Types
   Network Architecture
   Electronic Mail
   Electronic Commerce
       Electronic Funds Transfer
       Electronic Data Interchange
       Digital Signatures
       Electronic Signatures
   Access Controls (e.g., firewalls, proxy servers, dedicated circuits)
   Monitoring
   Cryptography

5. INFORMATION SHARING

   The requirements for information sharing by an IT system with one or more other IT systems or applications, for information sharing to support multiple internal or external organizations, missions, or public programs.

   Communications Types
   Network Architecture
   Electronic Mail
   Electronic Commerce
       Electronic Funds Transfer
       Electronic Data Interchange
       Digital Signatures
       Electronic Signatures
   Access Controls (e.g., Firewalls, Proxy servers, Dedicated circuits)
   Monitoring
   Cryptography
   Data Ownership
   Protection and Labeling of Data Storage Media

Exhibit 4-4 (Continued)
IT Security Body of Knowledge Topics and Concepts

6. SENSITIVITY

An IT environment consists of the system, data, and applications which must be examined individually and in total. All IT systems and applications require some level of protection (to ensure confidentiality, integrity, and availability) which is determined by an evaluation of the sensitivity and criticality of the information processed, the relation of the system to the organization missions and the economic value of the system components.

- Confidentiality
- Integrity
- Availability
- Criticality
- Aggregation

7. RISK MANAGEMENT

The on-going process of assessing the risk to IT resources and information, as part of a risk-based approach used to determine adequate security for a system, by analyzing the threats and vulnerabilities and selecting appropriate cost-effective controls to achieve and maintain an acceptable level of risk.

- Risk Assessment
- Risk Analysis
- Risk Mitigation
- Uncertainty Analysis
- Threats
- Vulnerabilities
- Risks
- Probability Estimation
- Rate of Occurrence
- Asset Valuation
- Adequate and Appropriate Protection of Assets
- Cost Effectiveness
- Cost-Benefit Analysis
- Application Security Reviews/Audits
- System Security Reviews/Audits
- Verification Reviews
- Internal Control Reviews
- EDP Audits

Information Technology Security Training Requirements

Exhibit 4-4 (Continued)
IT Security Body of Knowledge Topics and Concepts

8. MANAGEMENT CONTROLS

   Management controls are actions taken to manage the development, maintenance, and use of the system, including system-specific policies, procedures, and rules of behavior, individual roles and responsibilities, individual accountability and personnel security decisions.

   System/Application Responsibilities
       Program and Functional Managers
       Owners
       Custodians
       Contractors
       Related Security Program Managers
       IT System Security Manager
       Users
   System/Application-Specific Policies and Procedures
   Standard Operating Procedures
   Personnel Security
       Background Investigations
       Position Sensitivity
       Separation of Duties/Compartmentalization
   System Rules of Behavior
       Assignment and Limitation of System Privileges
       Connection to Other Systems and Networks
       Intellectual Property/Copyright Issues
       Remote Access/Work at Home Issues
       Official vs. Unofficial System Use
       Individual Accountability
   Sanctions or Penalties for Violations

9. ACQUISITION/DEVELOPMENT/INSTALLATION/IMPLEMENTATION CONTROLS

   The process of assuring that adequate controls are considered, evaluated, selected, designed and built into the system during its early planning and development stages and that an on-going process is established to ensure continued operation at an acceptable level of risk during the installation, implementation and operation stages.

   Life Cycle Planning
   Security Activities in Life Cycle Stages
   Security Plan Development and Maintenance
   Security Specifications
   Configuration Management
   Change Control Procedures
   Design Review and Testing
   Authority to Operate
       Certification/Recertification
       Accreditation/Re-accreditation
   Acquisition Specifications
   Contracts, Agreements and Other Obligations
   Acceptance Testing
   Prototyping

Information Technology Security Training Requirements

Exhibit 4-4 (Continued)
IT Security Body of Knowledge Topics and Concepts

10. OPERATIONAL CONTROLS

The day-to-day procedures and mechanisms used to protect operational systems and applications. Operational controls affect the system and application environment.

    Physical and Environmental Protection
        Physical Security Program
        Environmental Controls
        Natural Threats
        Facility Management
        Fire Prevention and Protection
        Electrical/Power
        Housekeeping
        Physical Access Controls
        Intrusion Detection/Alarms
        Maintenance
        Water/Plumbing
        Mobile and Portable, Systems
    Production, Input/Output Controls
        Document Labeling, Handling, Shipping and Storing
        Media Labeling, Handling, Shipping and Storing
        Disposal of Sensitive Material
        Magnetic Remnance - Cleaning and Clearing
    Contingency Planning
        Backups
        Contingency/Disaster Recovery Plan Development
        Contingency/Disaster Recovery Plan Testing
        Contracting for Contingency Services
        Contracting for Disaster Recovery Services
        Insurance/Government Self-Insurance
    Audit and Variance Detection
        System Logs and Records
        Deviations from Standard Activity
    Hardware and System Software Maintenance Controls
    Application Software Maintenance Controls
    Documentation

11. AWARENESS, TRAINING, AND EDUCATION CONTROLS

(1) *Awareness* programs set the stage for training by changing organizational attitudes to realize the importance of security and the adverse consequences of its failure. (2) The purpose of *training* is to teach people the skills that will enable them to perform their jobs more effectively. (3) *Education* is targeted for IT security professionals and focuses on developing the ability and vision to perform complex, multi-disciplinary activities.

Exhibit 4-4 (Continued)
IT Security Body of Knowledge Topics and Concepts

12. TECHNICAL CONTROLS

Technical controls consist of hardware and software controls used to provide automated protection to the IT system or applications. Technical controls operate within the technical system and applications.

    User Identification and Authentication
        Passwords
        Tokens
        Biometrics
        Single Log-in
    Authorization/Access Controls
        Logical Access Controls
        Role-Based Access
        System/Application Privileges
    Integrity/Validation Controls
        Compliance with Security Specifications and Requirements
        Malicious Program/Virus Protection, Detection and Removal
        Authentication Messages
        Reconciliation Routines
    Audit Trail Mechanisms
        Transaction Monitoring
        Reconstruction of Transactions
    Confidentiality Controls
        Cryptography
    Incident Response
        Fraud, Waste or Abuse
        Hackers and Unauthorized User Activities
        Incident Reporting
        Incident Investigation
        Prosecution
    Public Access Controls
        Access Controls
        Need-to-know
        Privileges
    Control Objectives
        Protection Requirements

Information Technology Security Training Requirements

SECTION
4.2

**IT SECURITY TRAINING
MATRIX CELLS**

(See Appendix B for a full-page illustration of the IT Security Training Matrix)

SECTION
4.2.1

**TRAINING AREA:
LAWS AND REGULATIONS**

INFORMATION TECHNOLOGY SECURITY TRAINING MATRIX — **Cell 1A**
Training Area: **Laws & Regulations** Functional Specialty: **Manage**
Definition — Federal government-wide and organization-specific published documents (laws, regulations, policies, guidelines, standards, and codes of conduct) governing mandated requirements and standards for the management and protection of information technology resources.
Behavioral Outcome — Managers are able to understand applicable governing documents and their interrelationships and interpret and apply them to the manager's area of responsibility.
Knowledge Levels — 1. Beginning — Research, Know, Identify 2. Intermediate — Analyze, Understand, Apply 3. Advanced — Interpret, Approve, Decide, Issue
Sample Learning Objectives — At the conclusion of this module, individuals will be able to: 1. Beginning — Know where to find Federal government-wide and organization-specific published documents, such as laws, regulations, policies, guidelines, and standards (e.g., the Computer Security Act of 1987) and how to apply them. 2. Intermediate — Develop policies that reflect the legislative intent of applicable laws and regulations (e.g., policies addressing software copyright law infringement). 3. Advanced — Analyze, approve, and issue policies (e.g., authorizes policies as part of an IRM manual).
Sample Job Functions — • Chief Information Officer (CIO) • Information Resources Management (IRM) Official, Senior • Information Resources Manager • IT Security Officer/Manager

Information Technology Security Training Requirements

INFORMATION TECHNOLOGY SECURITY TRAINING MATRIX — **Cell 1A**

Training Area: **Laws & Regulations**
Functional Specialty: **Manage**

IT SECURITY BODY OF KNOWLEDGE TOPICS AND CONCEPTS

- 1 — LAWS AND REGULATIONS
- 2 — IT SECURITY PROGRAM
- 7 — RISK MANAGEMENT

For the content of the numbered topics and concepts above, refer to ***Exhibit 4-4***.

INFORMATION TECHNOLOGY SECURITY TRAINING MATRIX — **Cell 1B**
Training Area: **Laws & Regulations** Functional Specialty: **Acquire**
Definition — Federal government-wide and organization-specific published documents (laws, regulations, policies, guidelines, standards, and codes of conduct) governing mandated requirements and standards for the management and protection of information technology resources.
Behavioral Outcome — Individuals involved in the acquisition of information technology resources have a sufficient understanding of IT security requirements and issues to protect the government's interest in such acquisitions.
Knowledge Levels — 1. Beginning —Identify, Know, Research 2. Intermediate — Analyze, Interpret, Develop, Decide 3. Advanced — Evaluate, Approve, Issue
Sample Learning Objectives — At the conclusion of this module, individuals will be able to: 1. Beginning — Identify security requirements to be included in statements of work and other appropriate procurement documents (e.g., procurement requests, purchase orders, task orders, and proposal evaluation summaries) as required by the Federal regulations. 2. Intermediate — Develop security requirements specific to an information technology acquisition for inclusion in procurement documents (e.g., ensures that required controls are adequate and appropriate) as required by the Federal regulations. 3. Advanced — Evaluate proposals to determine if proposed security solutions effectively address agency requirements as detailed in solicitation documents and are in compliance with Federal regulations.
Sample Job Functions — • Contracting Officer • Contracting Officer's Technical Representative (COTR) • Information Resources Management (IRM) Official, Senior • IT Security Officer/Manager • Source Selection Board Member

INFORMATION TECHNOLOGY SECURITY TRAINING MATRIX — **Cell 1B**

Training Area: **Laws & Regulations**
Functional Specialty: **Acquire**

IT SECURITY BODY OF KNOWLEDGE TOPICS AND CONCEPTS

- 1 — LAWS AND REGULATIONS
- 3 — SYSTEM ENVIRONMENT
- 5 — INFORMATION SHARING
- 6 — SENSITIVITY
- 7 — RISK MANAGEMENT
- 8 — MANAGEMENT CONTROLS
- 9 — ACQUISITION/DEVELOPMENT/INSTALLATION/ IMPLEMENTATION CONTROLS

*For the content of the numbered topics and concepts above, refer to **Exhibit 4-4**.*

INFORMATION TECHNOLOGY SECURITY TRAINING MATRIX — **Cell 1C**
Training Area: **Laws & Regulations** Functional Specialty: **Design & Develop**
Definition — Federal government-wide and organization-specific published documents (laws, regulations, policies, guidelines, standards, and codes of conduct) governing mandated requirements and standards for the management and protection of information technology resources.
Behavioral Outcome — Individuals responsible for the design and development of automated information systems are able to translate IT laws and regulations into technical specifications which provide adequate and appropriate levels of protection.
Knowledge Levels — 1. Beginning — Identify, Know, Apply 2. Intermediate — Research, Interpret, Develop 3. Advanced — Evaluate, Approve, Select
Sample Learning Objectives — At the conclusion of this module, individuals will be able to: 1. Beginning — Identify laws and regulations relevant to the specific system being designed (e.g., a financial management system would be subject to the requirements of the Accounting and Auditing Act, whereas a personnel system would be subject to the requirements of the Privacy Act). 2. Intermediate — Interpret applicable laws and regulations to develop security functional requirements (e.g., requiring encryption for Privacy Act data stored on a shared file server). 3. Advanced — Evaluate conflicting functional requirements (e.g., the level of audit trail that can be incorporated without adversely affecting system performance) and select for implementation those requirements that will provide the highest level of security at the minimum cost consistent with applicable laws and regulations.
Sample Job Functions — • Auditor, Internal • Program Manager • Information Resources Manager • Programmer/Systems Analyst • IT Security Officer/Manager • System Designer/Developer

Information Technology Security Training Requirements

INFORMATION TECHNOLOGY SECURITY TRAINING MATRIX — **Cell 1C**

Training Area: **Laws & Regulations**
Functional Specialty: **Design & Develop**

IT SECURITY BODY OF KNOWLEDGE TOPICS AND CONCEPTS

- 1 — LAWS AND REGULATIONS

- 2 — IT SECURITY PROGRAM

- 3 — SYSTEM ENVIRONMENT

- 4 — SYSTEM INTERCONNECTION

- 5 — INFORMATION SHARING

- 6 — SENSITIVITY

- 9 — ACQUISITION/DEVELOPMENT/INSTALLATION/ IMPLEMENTATION CONTROLS

For the content of the numbered topics and concepts above, refer to ***Exhibit 4-4****.*

INFORMATION TECHNOLOGY SECURITY TRAINING MATRIX — **Cell 1D**
Training Area: **Laws & Regulations** Functional Specialty: **Implement & Operate**
Definition — Federal government-wide and organization-specific published documents (laws, regulations, policies, guidelines, standards, and codes of conduct) governing mandated requirements and standards for the management and protection of information technology resources.
Behavioral Outcome — Individuals responsible for the technical implementation and daily operations of an automated information system are able to understand IT security laws and regulations in sufficient detail to ensure that appropriate safeguards are in place and enforced.
Knowledge Levels — 1. Beginning — Know, Identify, Apply 2. Intermediate — Investigate, Interpret, Decide, Analyze 3. Advanced — Evaluate, Decide, Approve
Sample Learning Objectives — At the conclusion of this module, individuals will be able to: 1. Beginning — Recognize a potential security violation and take appropriate action to report the incident as required by Federal regulation and mitigate any adverse impact (e.g., block access to a communications port which has been subject to multiple invalid log-on attempts during non-duty hours). 2. Intermediate — Investigate a potential security violation to determine if the organization's policy has been breached and assess the impact of the breach (e.g., review audit trails to determine if inappropriate access has occurred). 3. Advanced — Determine whether a security breach is indicative of a violation of law that requires specific legal action (e.g., unauthorized access and alteration of data) and forward evidence to the Federal Bureau of Investigation for investigation.
Sample Job Functions — • IT Security Officer/Manager   • Systems Operations Personnel • Programmer/Systems Analyst   • Technical Support Personnel • System Administrator   • Network Administrator

INFORMATION TECHNOLOGY SECURITY TRAINING MATRIX — **Cell 1D**
Training Area: **Laws & Regulations** Functional Specialty: **Implement & Operate**
IT SECURITY BODY OF KNOWLEDGE TOPICS AND CONCEPTS • 1 — LAWS AND REGULATIONS • 7 — RISK MANAGEMENT • 8 — MANAGEMENT CONTROLS • 10 — OPERATIONAL CONTROLS • 12 — TECHNICAL CONTROLS   *For the content of the numbered topics and concepts above, refer to **Exhibit 4-4**.*

INFORMATION TECHNOLOGY SECURITY TRAINING MATRIX — Cell 1E

Training Area: Laws & Regulations
Functional Specialty: Review & Evaluate

Definition —	Federal government-wide and organization-specific published documents (laws, regulations, policies, guidelines, standards, and codes of conduct) governing mandated requirements and standards for the management and protection of information technology resources.
Behavioral Outcome —	Individuals responsible for the review/evaluation of an automated information system are able to use IT security laws and regulations in developing a comparative baseline and determining the level of system compliance.

Knowledge Levels —

1. Beginning — Identify, Know, Apply
2. Intermediate — Develop, Interpret, Understand
3. Advanced — Evaluate, Decide, Approve

Sample Learning Objectives —

At the conclusion of this module, individuals will be able to:

1. Beginning — Identify laws and regulations applicable to a specific information system or application (e.g., a payroll application is subject to OMB Circulars A-123, A-127, and A-130, while a project management system may only be subject to OMB Circular A-130).

2. Intermediate — Use laws, regulations, and agency guidance to develop a comparative IT security requirements baseline appropriate to evaluate the existing security environment.

3. Advanced — Evaluate in-place controls and countermeasures against the comparative baseline to determine if the controls provide a security environment equal to or better than the baseline environment.

Sample Job Functions —

- Auditor, External
- Auditor, Internal
- Certification Reviewer
- Information Resources Manager
- IT Security Officer/Manager

Information Technology Security Training Requirements

INFORMATION TECHNOLOGY SECURITY TRAINING MATRIX — **Cell 1E**
Training Area: **Laws & Regulations** Functional Specialty: **Review & Evaluate**

IT SECURITY BODY OF KNOWLEDGE TOPICS AND CONCEPTS

- 1 — LAWS AND REGULATIONS
- 3 — SYSTEM ENVIRONMENT
- 4 — SYSTEM INTERCONNECTION
- 5 — INFORMATION SHARING
- 6 — SENSITIVITY
- 7 — RISK MANAGEMENT
- 8 — MANAGEMENT CONTROLS
- 9 — ACQUISITION/DEVELOPMENT/INSTALLATION/ IMPLEMENTATION CONTROLS
- 10 — OPERATIONAL CONTROLS
- 11 — AWARENESS, TRAINING, AND EDUCATION CONTROLS
- 12 — TECHNICAL CONTROLS

For the content of the numbered topics and concepts above, refer to ***Exhibit 4-4****.*

INFORMATION TECHNOLOGY SECURITY TRAINING MATRIX — **Cell 1F**
Training Area: **Laws & Regulations** Functional Specialty: **Use**
Definition — Federal government-wide and organization-specific published documents (laws, regulations, policies, guidelines, standards, and codes of conduct) governing mandated requirements and standards for the management and protection of information technology resources.
Behavioral Outcome — Users understand individual accountability and applicable governing documents (e.g., Computer Security Act, Computer Fraud and Abuse Act, Copyright Act, Privacy Act).
Knowledge Levels — 1. Beginning — Know, Apply 2. Intermediate/Advanced — Review, Assess, Decide
Sample Learning Objectives — At the conclusion of this module, individuals will be able to: 1. Beginning — Understand that violating applicable laws and regulations (e.g., making unauthorized copies of copyrighted software) can result in assessment of monetary penalties against individuals and the organization. 2. Intermediate/Advanced — Review personal practices to ensure compliance with applicable laws and regulations (e.g., review installed software on the computer for which he or she is responsible to ensure that each software product has an appropriate license).
Sample Job Functions — • Information Resources Manager • IT Security Officer/Manager • System Owner • User

Information Technology Security Training Requirements

INFORMATION TECHNOLOGY SECURITY TRAINING MATRIX — Cell 1F

Training Area: Laws & Regulations
Functional Specialty: Use

IT SECURITY BODY OF KNOWLEDGE TOPICS AND CONCEPTS

- 1 — LAWS AND REGULATIONS

- 8 — MANAGEMENT CONTROLS

For the content of the numbered topics and concepts above, refer to ***Exhibit 4-4***.

SECTION
4.2.2

**TRAINING AREA:
SECURITY PROGRAM**

INFORMATION TECHNOLOGY SECURITY TRAINING MATRIX — Cell 2.1A

Training Area: **Security Program — Planning**
Functional Specialty: **Manage**

Definition — The design and establishment of organizational structures and processes for IT security program goal-setting, prioritizing, and related decision-making activities; these encompass such elements as organization-specific scope and content, including: policy, guidelines, needs identification, roles, responsibilities, and resource allocation.

Behavioral Outcome — Individuals involved in the management of IT security programs are able to understand principles and processes of program planning and can organize resources to develop a security program that meets organizational needs.

Knowledge Levels —

1. Beginning — Participate, Know, Apply
2. Intermediate — Interpret, Develop, Decide
3. Advanced — Evaluate, Approve, Direct

Sample Learning Objectives —

At the conclusion of this module, individuals will be able to:

1. Beginning — Participate in the development or modification of the organization's IT security program plans and requirements.

2. Intermediate — Develop and/or modify IT security program policy, guidelines, and procedures and recommend associated resource allocations.

3. Advanced — Identify IT security program implications of new technologies or technology upgrades. Review and approve various IT security plans for appropriateness and effectiveness. Set priorities for allocation of resources.

Sample Job Functions —

- Information Resources Manager
- IT Security Officer/Manager
- Program Manager
- System Owner

Information Technology Security Training Requirements

INFORMATION TECHNOLOGY SECURITY TRAINING MATRIX — Cell 2.1A

Training Area: **Security Program — Planning**
Functional Specialty: **Manage**

IT SECURITY BODY OF KNOWLEDGE TOPICS AND CONCEPTS

- 1 — LAWS AND REGULATIONS
- 2 — IT SECURITY PROGRAM
- 3 — SYSTEM ENVIRONMENT
- 4 — SYSTEM INTERCONNECTION
- 5 — INFORMATION SHARING
- 6 — SENSITIVITY
- 7 — RISK MANAGEMENT
- 8 — MANAGEMENT CONTROLS
- 9 — ACQUISITION/DEVELOPMENT/INSTALLATION/ IMPLEMENTATION CONTROLS
- 10 — OPERATIONAL CONTROLS
- 11 — AWARENESS, TRAINING, AND EDUCATION CONTROLS
- 12 — TECHNICAL CONTROLS

For the content of the numbered topics and concepts above, refer to ***Exhibit 4-4***.

INFORMATION TECHNOLOGY SECURITY TRAINING MATRIX — **Cell 2.1B**
Training Area: **Security Program — Planning** Functional Specialty: **Acquire**
Definition — The design and establishment of organizational structures and processes for IT security program goal-setting, prioritizing, and related decision-making activities; these encompass such elements as organization-specific scope and content, including: policy, guidelines, needs identification, roles, responsibilities, and resource allocation.
Behavioral Outcome — Individuals involved in planning the IT security program can identify the resources required for successful implementation. Individuals recognize the need to include IT security requirements in IT acquisitions and to incorporate appropriate acquisition policy and oversight in the IT security program.
Knowledge Levels — 1. Beginning/Intermediate — Develop, Interpret, Decide, Apply 2. Advanced — Evaluate, Interpret, Approve, Issue
Sample Learning Objectives — At the conclusion of this module, individuals will be able to: 1. Beginning/Intermediate — Develop security requirements for hardware, software, and services acquisitions specific to the IT security program (e.g., purchase of virus-scanning software or security reviews) and for inclusion in general IT acquisition guidance. 2. Advanced — Interpret and/or approve security requirements relative to the capabilities of new information technologies, revise IT acquisition guidance as appropriate, and issue changes.
Sample Job Functions — • Contracting Officer's Technical Representative (COTR) • Information Resources Manager • IT Security Officer/Manager • Source Selection Board Member • Telecommunications Specialist

Information Technology Security Training Requirements

INFORMATION TECHNOLOGY SECURITY TRAINING MATRIX — **Cell 2.1B**
Training Area: **Security Program — Planning** Functional Specialty: **Acquire**

IT SECURITY BODY OF KNOWLEDGE TOPICS AND CONCEPTS

- 2 — IT SECURITY PROGRAM
- 3 — SYSTEM ENVIRONMENT
- 4 — SYSTEM INTERCONNECTION
- 5 — INFORMATION SHARING
- 9 — ACQUISITION/DEVELOPMENT/INSTALLATION/ IMPLEMENTATION CONTROLS
- 10 — OPERATIONAL CONTROLS
- 12 — TECHNICAL CONTROLS

For the content of the numbered topics and concepts above, refer to ***Exhibit 4-4****.*

INFORMATION TECHNOLOGY SECURITY TRAINING MATRIX — **Cell 2.1C**
Training Area: **Security Program — Planning** Functional Specialty: **Design & Develop**
Definition — The design and establishment of organizational structures and processes for IT security program goal-setting, prioritizing, and related decision-making activities; these encompass such elements as organization-specific scope and content, including: policy, guidelines, needs identification, roles, responsibilities, and resource allocation.
Behavioral Outcome — Individuals responsible for the design and development of an IT security program are able to create a security program plan specific to a business process or organizational entity.
Knowledge Levels — 1. Beginning — Locate, Understand, Apply 2. Intermediate/Advanced — Design, Develop, Decide
Sample Learning Objectives — At the conclusion of this module, individuals will be able to: 1. Beginning — Understand the various components of an effective IT security program and relate them to the organization's business process requirements. 2. Intermediate/Advanced — Design, develop, or modify IT security program requirements.
Sample Job Functions — • Chief Information Officer (CIO) • Information Resources Manager • IT Security Officer/Manager

INFORMATION TECHNOLOGY SECURITY TRAINING MATRIX — Cell 2.1C

Training Area: **Security Program — Planning**
Functional Specialty: **Design & Develop**

IT SECURITY BODY OF KNOWLEDGE TOPICS AND CONCEPTS

- 2 — IT SECURITY PROGRAM
- 3 — SYSTEM ENVIRONMENT
- 4 — SYSTEM INTERCONNECTION
- 5 — INFORMATION SHARING
- 6 — SENSITIVITY
- 7 — RISK MANAGEMENT
- 8 — MANAGEMENT CONTROLS
- 9 — ACQUISITION/DEVELOPMENT/INSTALLATION/ IMPLEMENTATION CONTROLS
- 10 — OPERATIONAL CONTROLS
- 11 — AWARENESS, TRAINING, AND EDUCATION CONTROLS
- 12 — TECHNICAL CONTROLS

For the content of the numbered topics and concepts above, refer to ***Exhibit 4-4***.

INFORMATION TECHNOLOGY SECURITY TRAINING MATRIX — **Cell 2.1D**
Training Area: **Security Program — Planning** Functional Specialty: **Implement & Operate**

Definition —	The design and establishment of organizational structures and processes for IT security program goal-setting, prioritizing, and related decision-making activities; these encompass such elements as organization-specific scope and content, including: policy, guidelines, needs identification, roles, responsibilities, and resource allocation.
Behavioral Outcome —	Individuals responsible for implementing and operating an IT security program are able to develop plans for security controls, countermeasures, and processes as required to execute the existing program.

Knowledge Levels —

1. Beginning — Understand, Participate, Develop, Apply
2. Intermediate/Advanced — Approve, Allocate, Interpret, Direct

Sample Learning Objectives —

At the conclusion of this module, individuals will be able to:

1. Beginning — Participate in the development of plans for implementing IT security program elements (e.g., develop procedures for screening new employees).

2. Intermediate/Advanced — Develop implementation strategies and resource estimates required to achieve IT security goals. Allocate resources among competing tasks to achieve the maximum level of security at optimum cost.

Sample Job Functions —

- Auditor, Internal
- Chief Information Officer (CIO)
- Information Resources Manager
- IT Security Officer/Manager

Information Technology Security Training Requirements

INFORMATION TECHNOLOGY SECURITY TRAINING MATRIX — Cell 2.1D

Training Area: **Security Program — Planning**
Functional Specialty: **Implement & Operate**

IT SECURITY BODY OF KNOWLEDGE TOPICS AND CONCEPTS

- 2 — IT SECURITY PROGRAM

- 7 — RISK MANAGEMENT

- 8 — MANAGEMENT CONTROLS

- 9 — ACQUISITION/DEVELOPMENT/INSTALLATION/ IMPLEMENTATION CONTROLS

- 10 — OPERATIONAL CONTROLS

- 11 — AWARENESS, TRAINING, AND EDUCATION CONTROLS

- 12 — TECHNICAL CONTROLS

*For the content of the numbered topics and concepts above, refer to **Exhibit 4-4**.*

INFORMATION TECHNOLOGY SECURITY TRAINING MATRIX — Cell 2.1E

Training Area: Security Program — Planning
Functional Specialty: Review & Evaluate

Definition — The design and establishment of organizational structures and processes for IT security program goal-setting, prioritizing, and related decision-making activities; these encompass such elements as organization-specific scope and content, including: policy, guidelines, needs identification, roles, responsibilities, and resource allocation.

Behavioral Outcome — Individuals responsible for the review/evaluation of an IT security program are able to review the program to determine its continuing capability to cost-effectively address identified requirements.

Knowledge Levels —

1. Beginning/Intermediate — Review, Know, Interpret
2. Advanced — Evaluate, Approve, Recommend

Sample Learning Objectives —

At the conclusion of this module, individuals will be able to:

1. Beginning/Intermediate — Review the plans for implementing IT security program elements to ensure that they effectively address program objectives.

2. Advanced — Provide recommendations for correcting identified deficiencies. Evaluate action plans for correcting identified deficiencies and provide recommendations for strengthening the IT security program plans.

Sample Job Functions —

- Auditor, External
- Auditor, Internal
- CIO
- Information Resources Management (IRM) Official, Senior
- IT Security Officer/Manager

Information Technology Security Training Requirements

INFORMATION TECHNOLOGY SECURITY TRAINING MATRIX — Cell 2.1E

Training Area: **Security Program — Planning**
Functional Specialty: **Review & Evaluate**

IT SECURITY BODY OF KNOWLEDGE TOPICS AND CONCEPTS

- 1 — LAWS AND REGULATIONS
- 2 — IT SECURITY PROGRAM
- 3 — SYSTEM ENVIRONMENT
- 4 — SYSTEM INTERCONNECTION
- 5 — INFORMATION SHARING
- 6 — SENSITIVITY
- 7 — RISK MANAGEMENT
- 8 — MANAGEMENT CONTROLS
- 9 — ACQUISITION/DEVELOPMENT/INSTALLATION/ IMPLEMENTATION CONTROLS
- 10 — OPERATIONAL CONTROLS
- 11 — AWARENESS, TRAINING, AND EDUCATION CONTROLS
- 12 — TECHNICAL CONTROLS

For the content of the numbered topics and concepts above, refer to **Exhibit 4-4**.

INFORMATION TECHNOLOGY SECURITY TRAINING MATRIX — Cell 2.2A

Training Area: Security Program — Management
Functional Specialty: Manage

Definition — The implementation and use of organizational structures and processes for IT security program goal-setting, prioritizing, and related decision-making activities; these encompass such elements as organization-specific policies, guidelines, requirements, roles, responsibilities, and resource allocation.

Behavioral Outcome — Individuals involved in IT security program management understand and are able to implement a security program that meets their organization's needs.

Knowledge Levels —

1. Beginning — Recognize, Know, Apply
2. Intermediate — Evaluate, Know, Review
3. Advanced — Determine, Interpret, Direct

Sample Learning Objectives —

At the conclusion of this module, individuals will be able to:

1. Beginning — Monitor organizational activities to ensure compliance with the existing IT security program (e.g., ensure that all IT systems have been identified and security plans prepared).

2. Intermediate — Review organizational IT security plans to ensure that they appropriately address the security requirements of each system.

3. Advanced — Interpret patterns of non-compliance to determine their impact on levels of risk and/or overall effectiveness of the IT security program and, on that basis, modify or augment the program as appropriate.

Sample Job Functions —

- Chief Information Officer (CIO)
- Information Resources Manager
- IT Security Officer/Manager
- Program Manager

INFORMATION TECHNOLOGY SECURITY TRAINING MATRIX — Cell 2.2A

Training Area: **Security Program — Management**
Functional Specialty: **Manage**

IT SECURITY BODY OF KNOWLEDGE TOPICS AND CONCEPTS

- 1 — LAWS AND REGULATIONS
- 2 — IT SECURITY PROGRAM
- 3 — SYSTEM ENVIRONMENT
- 4 — SYSTEM INTERCONNECTION
- 5 — INFORMATION SHARING
- 6 — SENSITIVITY
- 7 — RISK MANAGEMENT
- 8 — MANAGEMENT CONTROLS
- 9 — ACQUISITION/DEVELOPMENT/INSTALLATION/ IMPLEMENTATION CONTROLS
- 10 — OPERATIONAL CONTROLS
- 11 — AWARENESS, TRAINING, AND EDUCATION CONTROLS
- 12 — TECHNICAL CONTROLS

For the content of the numbered topics and concepts above, refer to ***Exhibit 4-4***.

INFORMATION TECHNOLOGY SECURITY TRAINING MATRIX — Cell 2.2B

Training Area: **Security Program — Management**
Functional Specialty: **Acquire**

Definition — The implementation and use of organizational structures and processes for IT security program goal-setting, prioritizing, and related decision-making activities; these encompass such elements as organization-specific policies, guidelines, requirements, roles, responsibilities, and resource allocation.

Behavioral Outcome — Individuals involved in managing the IT security program have a sufficient understanding of IT security and the acquisition process to incorporate IT security program requirements into acquisition work steps.

Knowledge Levels —

1. Beginning — Identify, Know, Apply
2. Intermediate — Define, Develop, Write
3. Advanced — Evaluate, Determine, Approve

Sample Learning Objectives —

At the conclusion of this module, individuals will be able to:

1. Beginning — Identify areas within the acquisition process where IT security work steps are required.

2. Intermediate — Develop security work steps for inclusion in the acquisition process, e.g., requiring an IT Security Officer review of statements of work.

3. Advanced — Evaluate procurement activities to ensure that IT security work steps are being effectively performed.

Sample Job Functions —

- Contracting Officer
- Contracting Officer's Technical Representative (COTR)
- Information Resources Manager
- IT Security Officer/Manager
- Source Selection Board Member

Information Technology Security Training Requirements

INFORMATION TECHNOLOGY SECURITY TRAINING MATRIX — **Cell 2.2B**

Training Area: **Security Program — Management**
Functional Specialty: **Acquire**

IT SECURITY BODY OF KNOWLEDGE TOPICS AND CONCEPTS

- 1 — LAWS AND REGULATIONS

- 2 — IT SECURITY PROGRAM

- 3 — SYSTEM ENVIRONMENT

- 9 — ACQUISITION/DEVELOPMENT/INSTALLATION/ IMPLEMENTATION CONTROLS

For the content of the numbered topics and concepts above, refer to **Exhibit 4-4**.

INFORMATION TECHNOLOGY SECURITY TRAINING MATRIX — **Cell 2.2C**
Training Area: **Security Program — Management** Functional Specialty: **Design & Develop**

Definition —	The implementation and use of organizational structures and processes for IT security program goal-setting, prioritizing, and related decision-making activities; these encompass such elements as organization-specific policies, guidelines, requirements, roles, responsibilities, and resource allocation.
Behavioral Outcome —	Individuals responsible for the design and development of an IT security program have sufficient understanding of the appropriate program elements and requirements to be able to translate them into detailed policies and procedures which provide adequate and appropriate protection for the organization's IT resources in relation to acceptable levels of risk.

Knowledge Levels —

1. Beginning — Know, Research, Understand
2. Intermediate — Interpret, Decide, Establish, Apply
3. Advanced — Analyze, Interpret, Approve, Direct

Sample Learning Objectives —

At the conclusion of this module, individuals will be able to:

1. Beginning — Understand categories of risk and participate in the design and development of operational IT security program procedures.

2. Intermediate — Establish acceptable levels of risk and translate the IT security program elements into operational procedures for providing adequate and appropriate protection of the organization's IT resources.

3. Advanced — Design, develop, and direct the activities necessary to marshal the organizational structures, processes, and people for an effective IT security program implementation.

Sample Job Functions —

- Chief Information Officer (CIO)
- Information Resources Management (IRM) Official, Senior
- IT Security Officer/Manager

INFORMATION TECHNOLOGY SECURITY TRAINING MATRIX — Cell 2.2C

Training Area: Security Program — Management
Functional Specialty: Design & Develop

IT SECURITY BODY OF KNOWLEDGE TOPICS AND CONCEPTS

- 2 — IT SECURITY PROGRAM

- 7 — RISK MANAGEMENT

- 9 — ACQUISITION/DEVELOPMENT/INSTALLATION/ IMPLEMENTATION CONTROLS

*For the content of the numbered topics and concepts above, refer to **Exhibit 4-4**.*

Information Technology Security Training Requirements

INFORMATION TECHNOLOGY SECURITY TRAINING MATRIX — Cell 2.2D
Training Area: **Security Program — Management** Functional Specialty: **Implement & Operate**
Definition — The implementation and use of organizational structures and processes for IT security program goal-setting, prioritizing, and related decision-making activities; these encompass such elements as organization-specific policies, guidelines, requirements, roles, responsibilities, and resource allocation.
Behavioral Outcome — Individuals who are responsible for the implementation and daily operations of an IT security program have a sufficient understanding of the appropriate program elements and requirements to be able to apply them in a manner which provides adequate and appropriate levels of protection for the organization's IT resources.
Knowledge Levels — 1. Beginning — Identify, Understand, Apply 2. Intermediate — Interpret, Analyze, Decide 3. Advanced — Investigate, Approve, Direct
Sample Learning Objectives — At the conclusion of this module, individuals will be able to: 1. Beginning — Apply organization-specific IT security program elements to the implementation of the program and identify areas of weakness. 2. Intermediate — Analyze patterns of non-compliance and take appropriate administrative or programmatic actions to minimize security risks. 3. Advanced — Direct the implementation of appropriate operational structures and processes to ensure an effective IT security program.
Sample Job Functions — • Information Resources Management (IRM) Official, Senior   • Program Manager • Information Resources Manager   • System Administrator • IT Security Officer/Manager   • System Owner • Network Administrator

INFORMATION TECHNOLOGY SECURITY TRAINING MATRIX — Cell 2.2D

Training Area: **Security Program — Management**
Functional Specialty: **Implement & Operate**

IT SECURITY BODY OF KNOWLEDGE TOPICS AND CONCEPTS

- 1 — LAWS AND REGULATIONS
- 2 — IT SECURITY PROGRAM
- 3 — SYSTEM ENVIRONMENT
- 4 — SYSTEM INTERCONNECTION
- 5 — INFORMATION SHARING
- 6 — SENSITIVITY
- 7 — RISK MANAGEMENT
- 8 — MANAGEMENT CONTROLS
- 9 — ACQUISITION/DEVELOPMENT/INSTALLATION/ IMPLEMENTATION CONTROLS
- 10 — OPERATIONAL CONTROLS
- 11 — AWARENESS, TRAINING, AND EDUCATION CONTROLS
- 12 — TECHNICAL CONTROLS

*For the content of the numbered topics and concepts above, refer to **Exhibit 4-4**.*

Information Technology Security Training Requirements

INFORMATION TECHNOLOGY SECURITY TRAINING MATRIX — Cell 2.2E Training Area: **Security Program —Management** Functional Specialty: **Review & Evaluate**
Definition — The implementation and use of organizational structures and processes for IT security program goal-setting, prioritizing, and related decision-making activities; these encompass such elements as organization-specific policies, guidelines, requirements, roles, responsibilities, and resource allocation.
Behavioral Outcome — Individuals responsible for the review/evaluation of an IT security program have an adequate understanding of IT security laws, regulations, standards, guidelines, and the organizational environment to determine if the program adequately addresses all threats and areas of potential vulnerability.
Knowledge Levels — 1. Beginning — Understand, Evaluate, Apply 2. Intermediate — Research, Compile, Interpret, Decide, Write 3. Advanced — Direct, Validate, Oversee
Sample Learning Objectives — At the conclusion of this module, individuals will be able to: 1. Beginning — Participate in the review of an organization's IT security program and evaluate the extent to the program is being managed effectively. 2. Intermediate — Develop compliance findings and recommendations. 3. Advanced — Direct the review of the management of an organization's IT security program, validate findings and recommendations, and establish follow-up monitoring for corrective actions.
Sample Job Functions — • Auditor, External • Auditor, Internal • Information Resources Management (IRM) Official, Senior • IT Security Officer/Manager

Chapter 4. Training Development Methodology

INFORMATION TECHNOLOGY SECURITY TRAINING MATRIX — Cell 2.2E

Training Area: Security Program — Management
Functional Specialty: Review & Evaluate

IT SECURITY BODY OF KNOWLEDGE TOPICS AND CONCEPTS

- 1 — LAWS AND REGULATIONS
- 2 — IT SECURITY PROGRAM
- 3 — SYSTEM ENVIRONMENT
- 4 — SYSTEM INTERCONNECTION
- 5 — INFORMATION SHARING
- 6 — SENSITIVITY
- 7 — RISK MANAGEMENT
- 8 — MANAGEMENT CONTROLS
- 9 — ACQUISITION/DEVELOPMENT/INSTALLATION/ IMPLEMENTATION CONTROLS
- 10 — OPERATIONAL CONTROLS
- 11 — AWARENESS, TRAINING, AND EDUCATION CONTROLS
- 12 — TECHNICAL CONTROLS

For the content of the numbered topics and concepts above, refer to **Exhibit 4-4**.

SECTION 4.2.3

**TRAINING AREA:
SYSTEM LIFE CYCLE SECURITY**

Information Technology Security Training Requirements

INFORMATION TECHNOLOGY SECURITY TRAINING MATRIX — Cell 3.1A

Training Area: **System Life Cycle Security — Initiation**
Functional Specialty: **Manage**

Definition — The system life cycle is a model for building and operating an IT system from its initial inception to its termination and disposal of assets. The model includes six phases: Initiation, Development, Test and Evaluation, Implementation, Operations, and Termination. Life cycle security is the ensemble of processes and procedures which ensures data confidentiality, as needed, as well as data and system integrity, and availability.

The initiation phase is the series of steps followed to ensure that security requirements are considered and resolved as new information systems and technologies are planned.

Behavioral Outcome — Individuals with management responsibilities are able to identify steps in the system development life cycle where security requirements and concerns (e.g., confidentiality, integrity, and availability) need to be considered and to define the processes to be used to resolve those concerns.

Knowledge Levels —

1. Beginning — Understand, Know, Recognize
2. Intermediate — Identify, Assess, Decide
3. Advanced — Analyze, Approve, Direct

Sample Learning Objectives —

At the conclusion of this module, individuals will be able to:

1. Beginning — Understand the need to plan security into new information systems from the beginning and the benefits to be derived from doing so.

2. Intermediate — Identify alternative functional IT security strategies to address system security concerns.

3. Advanced — Analyze identified IT security strategies and select those that are the best approach/practice.

Sample Job Functions —

- Information Resources Manager
- IT Security Officer/Manager
- Program Manager
- System Designer/Developer
- System Owner

Chapter 4. Training Development Methodology

Information Technology Security Training Requirements

INFORMATION TECHNOLOGY SECURITY TRAINING MATRIX — Cell 3.1A

Training Area: **System Life Cycle Security — Initiation**
Functional Specialty: **Manage**

IT SECURITY BODY OF KNOWLEDGE TOPICS AND CONCEPTS

- 2 — IT SECURITY PROGRAM
- 5 — INFORMATION SHARING
- 6 — SENSITIVITY
- 8 — MANAGEMENT CONTROLS
- 9 — ACQUISITION/DEVELOPMENT/INSTALLATION/ IMPLEMENTATION CONTROLS

*For the content of the numbered topics and concepts above, refer to **Exhibit 4-4**.*

INFORMATION TECHNOLOGY SECURITY TRAINING MATRIX — Cell 3.1B

Training Area: System Life Cycle Security — Initiation
Functional Specialty: Acquire

Definition — The system life cycle is a model for building and operating an IT system from its initial inception to its termination and disposal of assets. The model includes six phases: Initiation, Development, Test and Evaluation, Implementation, Operations, and Termination. Life cycle security is the ensemble of processes and procedures which ensures data confidentiality, as needed, as well as data and system integrity, and availability.

The initiation phase is the series of steps followed to ensure that security requirements are considered and resolved as new information systems and technologies are planned.

Behavioral Outcome — Individuals with acquisition responsibilities are able to analyze and develop acquisition documents and/or provide guidance which ensures that functional IT security requirements are incorporated.

Knowledge Levels —

1. Beginning — Identify, Locate, Understand
2. Intermediate — Develop, Research, Write
3. Advanced — Analyze, Evaluate, Approve

Sample Learning Objectives —

At the conclusion of this module, individuals will be able to:

1. Beginning — Identify general and system-specific IT security specifications which pertain to a particular system acquisition being planned.

2. Intermediate — Develop security-related portions of acquisition documents.

3. Advanced — Ensure that security-related portions of the system acquisition documents meet all identified security needs.

Sample Job Functions —

- Contracting Officer
- Contracting Officer's Technical Representative (COTR)
- IT Security Officer/Manager
- System Designer/Developer
- System Owner

> **INFORMATION TECHNOLOGY SECURITY TRAINING MATRIX — Cell 3.1B**
>
> Training Area: **System Life Cycle Security — Initiation**
> Functional Specialty: **Acquire**
>
> ## IT SECURITY BODY OF KNOWLEDGE TOPICS AND CONCEPTS
>
> - 2 — IT SECURITY PROGRAM
> - 3 — SYSTEM ENVIRONMENT
> - 4 — SYSTEM INTERCONNECTION
> - 5 — INFORMATION SHARING
> - 6 — SENSITIVITY
> - 9 — ACQUISITION/DEVELOPMENT/INSTALLATION/ IMPLEMENTATION CONTROLS
> - 10 — OPERATIONAL CONTROLS
> - 12 — TECHNICAL CONTROLS
>
> *For the content of the numbered topics and concepts above, refer to* ***Exhibit 4-4***.

INFORMATION TECHNOLOGY SECURITY TRAINING MATRIX — Cell 3.1C

Training Area: **System Life Cycle Security — Initiation**
Functional Specialty: **Design & Develop**

Definition — The system life cycle is a model for building and operating an IT system from its initial inception to its termination and disposal of assets. The model includes six phases: Initiation, Development, Test and Evaluation, Implementation, Operations, and Termination. Life cycle security is the ensemble of processes and procedures which ensures data confidentiality, as needed, as well as data and system integrity, and availability.

The initiation phase is the series of steps followed to ensure that security requirements are considered and resolved as new information systems and technologies are planned.

Behavioral Outcome — Individuals responsible for the design and development of IT systems are able to translate IT security requirements into system-level security specifications.

Knowledge Levels —

1. Beginning — Identify, Define, Participate
2. Intermediate — Understand, Interpret, Translate
3. Advanced — Analyze, Determine, Approve

Sample Learning Objectives —

At the conclusion of this module, individuals will be able to:

1. Beginning — Identify areas where specific IT security countermeasures are required and participate in the development of security strategies.

2. Intermediate — Translate IT security strategies into initial security specifications for the planned system.

3. Advanced — Approve IT security specifications for inclusion in the formal system baseline.

Sample Job Functions —

- IT Security Officer/Manager
- Program Manager
- System Designer/Developer
- System Owner

INFORMATION TECHNOLOGY SECURITY TRAINING MATRIX — **Cell 3.1C**

Training Area: **System Life Cycle Security — Initiation**
Functional Specialty: **Design & Develop**

IT SECURITY BODY OF KNOWLEDGE TOPICS AND CONCEPTS

- 2 — IT SECURITY PROGRAM
- 3 — SYSTEM ENVIRONMENT
- 4 — SYSTEM INTERCONNECTION
- 5 — INFORMATION SHARING
- 6 — SENSITIVITY
- 9 — ACQUISITION/DEVELOPMENT/INSTALLATION/ IMPLEMENTATION CONTROLS

*For the content of the numbered topics and concepts above, refer to **Exhibit 4-4**.*

Information Technology Security Training Requirements

INFORMATION TECHNOLOGY SECURITY TRAINING MATRIX — **Cell 3.1E**
Training Area: **System Life Cycle Security — Initiation** Functional Specialty: **Review & Evaluate**

Definition —	The system life cycle is a model for building and operating an IT system from its initial inception to its termination and disposal of assets. The model includes six phases: Initiation, Development, Test and Evaluation, Implementation, Operations, and Termination. Life cycle security is the ensemble of processes and procedures which ensures data confidentiality, as needed, as well as data and system integrity, and availability. The initiation phase is the series of steps followed to ensure that security requirements are considered and resolved as new information systems and technologies are planned.
Behavioral Outcome —	Individuals are able to evaluate planning documents associated with a particular system to ensure that appropriate IT security requirements have been considered and incorporated.

Knowledge Levels —

1. Beginning — Understand, Participate, Assess
2. Intermediate — Conduct, Research, Interpret
3. Advanced — Verify, Analyze, Recommend

Sample Learning Objectives —

At the conclusion of this module, individuals will be able to:

1. Beginning — Participate in the evaluation of functional IT security requirements for a system.

2. Intermediate — Conduct the review and evaluation of functional IT security requirements for a system.

3. Advanced — Verify that the security requirements for a system are appropriately incorporated into the system design.

Sample Job Functions —

- Auditor, External
- Auditor, Internal
- Information Resources Manager
- IT Security Officer/Manager
- System Owner

Chapter 4. Training Development Methodology

INFORMATION TECHNOLOGY SECURITY TRAINING MATRIX — **Cell 3.1E**
Training Area: **Laws & Regulations** Functional Specialty: **Review & Evaluate**

IT SECURITY BODY OF KNOWLEDGE TOPICS AND CONCEPTS

- 2 — IT SECURITY PROGRAM
- 3 — SYSTEM ENVIRONMENT
- 4 — SYSTEM INTERCONNECTION
- 5 — INFORMATION SHARING
- 6 — SENSITIVITY
- 7 — RISK MANAGEMENT
- 8 — MANAGEMENT CONTROLS
- 9 — ACQUISITION/DEVELOPMENT/INSTALLATION/ IMPLEMENTATION CONTROLS
- 10 — OPERATIONAL CONTROLS
- 11 — AWARENESS, TRAINING, AND EDUCATION CONTROLS
- 12 — TECHNICAL CONTROLS

*For the content of the numbered topics and concepts above, refer to **Exhibit 4-4**.*

INFORMATION TECHNOLOGY SECURITY TRAINING MATRIX — Cell 3.1F

Training Area: System Life Cycle Security — Initiation
Functional Specialty: Use

Definition — The system life cycle is a model for building and operating an IT system from its initial inception to its termination and disposal of assets. The model includes six phases: Initiation, Development, Test and Evaluation, Implementation, Operations, and Termination. Life cycle security is the ensemble of processes and procedures which ensures data confidentiality, as needed, as well as data and system integrity, and availability.

The initiation phase is the series of steps followed to ensure that security requirements are considered and resolved as new information systems and technologies are planned.

Behavioral Outcome — Potential users are able to participate in needs analyses and understand the various points of view involved in setting the balance between IT security controls and system efficiency.

Knowledge Levels —

1. Beginning — Understand, Identify
2. Intermediate/Advanced — Know, Analyze, Participate, Suggest

Sample Learning Objectives —

At the conclusion of this module, individuals will be able to:

1. Beginning — Participate in the identification of system confidentiality, integrity, and availability requirements in relation to user needs and risk management.

2. Intermediate/Advanced — Participate in the analysis and selection of security alternatives.

Sample Job Functions —

- IT Security Officer/Manager
- System Owner
- User

INFORMATION TECHNOLOGY SECURITY TRAINING MATRIX — Cell 3.1F

Training Area: **Laws & Regulations**
Functional Specialty: **Use**

IT SECURITY BODY OF KNOWLEDGE TOPICS AND CONCEPTS

- 2 — IT SECURITY PROGRAM
- 6 — SENSITIVITY
- 7 — RISK MANAGEMENT

For the content of the numbered topics and concepts above, refer to ***Exhibit 4-4****.*

INFORMATION TECHNOLOGY SECURITY TRAINING MATRIX — **Cell 3.2A**
Training Area: **System Life Cycle Security — Development** Functional Specialty: **Manage**
Definition — The system life cycle is a model for building and operating an IT system from its initial inception to its termination and disposal of assets. The model includes six phases: Initiation, Development, Test and Evaluation, Implementation, Operations, and Termination. Life cycle security is the ensemble of processes and procedures which ensures data confidentiality, as needed, as well as data and system integrity, and availability. The development phase is the series of steps followed to ensure that security requirements are considered, resolved, and incorporated as information systems and technologies are developed or changed.
Behavioral Outcome — Individuals with management responsibilities are able to ensure that the formal developmental baseline includes approved security requirements and that security-related features are installed, clearly identified, and documented.
Knowledge Levels — 1. Beginning — Understand, Know, Apply 2. Intermediate — Identify, Review, Decide 3. Advanced — Evaluate, Analyze, Approve
Sample Learning Objectives — At the conclusion of this module, individuals will be able to: 1. Beginning — Understand the relationship between planned security safeguards and the features being installed on the system under development. Provide input on security concerns during system development efforts. 2. Intermediate — Review the selected security safeguards to determine if security concerns identified in the approved plan have been fully addressed. 3. Advanced — Evaluate and approve development efforts to ensure that baseline security safeguards are appropriately installed for the system being developed or modified.
Sample Job Functions — • Information Resources Manager • IT Security Officer/Manager • System Designer/Developer • System Owner

INFORMATION TECHNOLOGY SECURITY TRAINING MATRIX — **Cell 3.2A**
Training Area: **System Life Cycle Security — Development** Functional Specialty: **Manage**

IT SECURITY BODY OF KNOWLEDGE TOPICS AND CONCEPTS

- 4 — SYSTEM INTERCONNECTION

- 5 — INFORMATION SHARING

- 6 — SENSITIVITY

- 7 — RISK MANAGEMENT

- 8 — MANAGEMENT CONTROLS

- 9 — ACQUISITION/DEVELOPMENT/INSTALLATION/ IMPLEMENTATION CONTROLS

For the content of the numbered topics and concepts above, refer to ***Exhibit 4-4***.

INFORMATION TECHNOLOGY SECURITY TRAINING MATRIX — Cell 3.2B

Training Area: **System Life Cycle Security — Development**
Functional Specialty: **Acquire**

Definition —	The system life cycle is a model for building and operating an IT system from its initial inception to its termination and disposal of assets. The model includes six phases: Initiation, Development, Test and Evaluation, Implementation, Operations, and Termination. Life cycle security is the ensemble of processes and procedures which ensures data confidentiality, as needed, as well as data and system integrity, and availability.
	The development phase is the series of steps followed to ensure that security requirements are considered, resolved, and incorporated as information systems and technologies are developed or changed.
Behavioral Outcome —	Individuals with acquisition responsibilities are able to monitor procurement actions to ensure that IT security requirements are satisfied.

Knowledge Levels —

1. Beginning — Identify, Know, Apply
2. Intermediate/Advanced — Evaluate, Analyze, Interpret

Sample Learning Objectives —

At the conclusion of this module, individuals will be able to:

1. Beginning — Ensure that IT security requirements are appropriately identified in acquisition documents.

2. Intermediate/Advanced — Evaluate the presence and adequacy of security measures proposed or provided in response to requirements contained in acquisition documents.

Sample Job Functions —

- Contracting Officer
- Contracting Officer's Technical Representative (COTR)
- IT Security Officer/Manager
- Source Selection Board Member
- System Owner

Information Technology Security Training Requirements

INFORMATION TECHNOLOGY SECURITY TRAINING MATRIX — **Cell 3.2B**
Training Area: **System Life Cycle Security — Development** Functional Specialty: **Acquire**

IT SECURITY BODY OF KNOWLEDGE TOPICS AND CONCEPTS

- 9 — ACQUISITION/DEVELOPMENT/INSTALLATION/ IMPLEMENTATION CONTROLS

For the content of the numbered topics and concepts above, refer to **Exhibit 4-4**.

Chapter 4. Training Development Methodology 108

INFORMATION TECHNOLOGY SECURITY TRAINING MATRIX — Cell 3.2C

Training Area: **System Life Cycle Security — Development**
Functional Specialty: **Design & Develop**

Definition — The system life cycle is a model for building and operating an IT system from its initial inception to its termination and disposal of assets. The model includes six phases: Initiation, Development, Test and Evaluation, Implementation, Operations, and Termination. Life cycle security is the ensemble of processes and procedures which ensures data confidentiality, as needed, as well as data and system integrity, and availability.

The development phase is the series of steps followed to ensure that security requirements are considered, resolved, and incorporated as information systems and technologies are developed or changed.

Behavioral Outcome — Individuals responsible for system design, development or modification are able to use baseline IT security requirements to select and install appropriate safeguards.

Knowledge Levels —

1. Beginning — Know, Construct, Apply
2. Intermediate — Identify, Recommend, Interpret
3. Advanced — Determine, Select, Approve

Sample Learning Objectives —

At the conclusion of this module, individuals will be able to:

1. Beginning — Participate in the construction of the IT system in accordance with the formal design specifications: developing manual procedures, using off-the-shelf hardware/software components, writing program code, customizing hardware components, and/or using other IT capabilities.

2. Intermediate — Identify and recommend alternative safeguards that will satisfy baseline security specifications.

3. Advanced — Review recommendations and select appropriate safeguards for implementation.

Sample Job Functions —

- Freedom of Information Act Official
- IT Security Officer/Manager
- System Designer/Developer
- Programmer/Systems Analyst
- Records Management Official
- Privacy Act Official

INFORMATION TECHNOLOGY SECURITY TRAINING MATRIX — **Cell 3.2C**
Training Area: **System Life Cycle Security — Development** Functional Specialty: **Design & Develop**

IT SECURITY BODY OF KNOWLEDGE TOPICS AND CONCEPTS

- 2 — IT SECURITY PROGRAM
- 3 — SYSTEM ENVIRONMENT
- 4 — SYSTEM INTERCONNECTION
- 5 — INFORMATION SHARING
- 6 — SENSITIVITY
- 7 — RISK MANAGEMENT
- 9 — ACQUISITION/DEVELOPMENT/INSTALLATION/ IMPLEMENTATION CONTROLS

*For the content of the numbered topics and concepts above, refer to **Exhibit 4-4**.*

INFORMATION TECHNOLOGY SECURITY TRAINING MATRIX — Cell 3.2D

Training Area: **System Life Cycle Security — Development**
Functional Specialty: **Implement & Operate**

Definition — The system life cycle is a model for building and operating an IT system from its initial inception to its termination and disposal of assets. The model includes six phases: Initiation, Development, Test and Evaluation, Implementation, Operations, and Termination. Life cycle security is the ensemble of processes and procedures which ensures data confidentiality, as needed, as well as data and system integrity, and availability.

The development phase is the series of steps followed to ensure that security requirements are considered, resolved, and incorporated as information systems and technologies are developed or changed.

Behavioral Outcome — Individuals responsible for system implementation or operation are able to assemble, integrate, and install systems so that the functionality and effectiveness of safeguards can be tested and evaluated.

Knowledge Levels —

1. Beginning — Install, Operate, Understand
2. Intermediate — Analyze, Approve, Recommend
3. Advanced — Direct, Require, Ensure

Sample Learning Objectives —

At the conclusion of this module, individuals will be able to:

1. Beginning — Install and operate the IT systems in a test configuration in a manner that does not alter the program code or compromise security safeguards.

2. Intermediate — Analyze system performance for potential security problems (e.g., failure to update access control tables, corrupted data).

3. Advanced — Provide direction to system developers regarding correction of security problems identified during testing.

Sample Job Functions —

- Data Center Manager
- Database Administrator
- IT Security Officer/Manager
- Network Administrator
- System Administrator
- System Designer/Developer
- System Operations Personnel
- Technical Support Personnel

INFORMATION TECHNOLOGY SECURITY TRAINING MATRIX — **Cell 3.2D**
Training Area: **System Life Cycle Security — Development** Functional Specialty: **Implement & Operate**

IT SECURITY BODY OF KNOWLEDGE TOPICS AND CONCEPTS

- 3 — SYSTEM ENVIRONMENT
- 4 — SYSTEM INTERCONNECTION
- 5 — INFORMATION SHARING
- 8 — MANAGEMENT CONTROLS
- 9 — ACQUISITION/DEVELOPMENT/INSTALLATION/ IMPLEMENTATION CONTROLS
- 10 — OPERATIONAL CONTROLS
- 12 — TECHNICAL CONTROLS

*For the content of the numbered topics and concepts above, refer to **Exhibit 4-4**.*

INFORMATION TECHNOLOGY SECURITY TRAINING MATRIX — **Cell 3.2E**
Training **Area: System Life Cycle Security — Development** Functional Specialty: **Review & Evaluate**
Definition — The system life cycle is a model for building and operating an IT system from its initial inception to its termination and disposal of assets. The model includes six phases: Initiation, Development, Test and Evaluation, Implementation, Operations, and Termination. Life cycle security is the ensemble of processes and procedures which ensures data confidentiality, as needed, as well as data and system integrity, and availability. The development phase is the series of steps followed to ensure that security requirements are considered, resolved, and incorporated as information systems and technologies are developed or changed.
Behavioral Outcome — Individuals responsible for review and evaluation are able to examine development efforts at specified milestones to ensure that approved safeguards are in place and documented.
Knowledge Levels — 1. Beginning — Know, Review, Evaluate 2. Intermediate/Advanced — Analyze, Recommend, Approve
Sample Learning Objectives — At the conclusion of this module, individuals will be able to: 1. Beginning — Review IT system development documents for inclusion of appropriate safeguards. 2. Intermediate — Review and evaluate IT system development documents to ensure that system safeguards, as a whole, result in an acceptable level of risk. 3. Advanced — Evaluate configuration controls, review development of security test plans and procedures, and ensure that security requirements are documented and comply with the formal design specification.
Sample Job Functions — • Auditor, External • Auditor, Internal • Certification Reviewer • Designated Approving Authority (DAA) • IT Security Officer/Manager • Program Manager • System Owner

INFORMATION TECHNOLOGY SECURITY TRAINING MATRIX — Cell 3.2E

Training Area: **System Life Cycle Security — Development**
Functional Specialty: **Review & Evaluate**

IT SECURITY BODY OF KNOWLEDGE TOPICS AND CONCEPTS

- 7 — RISK MANAGEMENT

- 8 — MANAGEMENT CONTROLS

- 9 — ACQUISITION/DEVELOPMENT/INSTALLATION/ IMPLEMENTATION CONTROLS

- 10 — OPERATIONAL CONTROLS

- 12 — TECHNICAL CONTROLS

*For the content of the numbered topics and concepts above, refer to **Exhibit 4-4**.*

INFORMATION TECHNOLOGY SECURITY TRAINING MATRIX — **Cell 3.2F**
Training Area: **System Life Cycle Security — Development** Functional Specialty: **Use**

Definition —	The system life cycle is a model for building and operating an IT system from its initial inception to its termination and disposal of assets. The model includes six phases: Initiation, Development, Test and Evaluation, Implementation, Operations, and Termination. Life cycle security is the ensemble of processes and procedures which ensures data confidentiality, as needed, as well as data and system integrity, and availability. The development phase is the series of steps followed to ensure that security requirements are considered, resolved, and incorporated as information systems and technologies are developed or changed.
Behavioral Outcome —	Potential users are able to provide input to system development efforts to ensure that IT security safeguards are as transparent to the user as feasible and are balanced with ease of use.

Knowledge Levels —

1. Beginning/Intermediate/Advanced — Understand, Know, Apply

Sample Learning Objectives —

At the conclusion of this module, individuals will be able to:

1. Beginning/Intermediate/Advanced — Appreciate the balance between operational efficiency, integrity, and availability for the system under development.

Sample Job Functions —

- IT Security Officer/Manager
- User

INFORMATION TECHNOLOGY SECURITY TRAINING MATRIX — Cell 3.2F

Training Area: **System Life Cycle Security — Development**
Functional Specialty: **Use**

IT SECURITY BODY OF KNOWLEDGE TOPICS AND CONCEPTS

- 6 — SENSITIVITY

- 8 — MANAGEMENT CONTROLS

*For the content of the numbered topics and concepts above, refer to **Exhibit 4-4**.*

INFORMATION TECHNOLOGY SECURITY TRAINING MATRIX — Cell 3.3C

Training Area: System Life Cycle Security — Test & Evaluate
Functional Specialty: Design & Develop

Definition — The system life cycle is a model for building and operating an IT system from its initial inception to its termination and disposal of assets. The model includes six phases: Initiation, Development, Test and Evaluation, Implementation, Operations, and Termination. Life cycle security is the ensemble of processes and procedures which ensures data confidentiality, as needed, as well as data and system integrity, and availability.

The test and evaluation phase is the series of steps followed to ensure that the design and construction of a new or modified information system or technology has successfully incorporated appropriate security safeguards.

Behavioral Outcome — Individuals are able to design tests to evaluate the adequacy of security safeguards in IT systems.

Knowledge Levels —

1. Beginning — Know, Design, Write
2. Intermediate — Analyze, Design, Develop
3. Advanced — Interpret, Evaluate, Approve

Sample Learning Objectives —

At the conclusion of this module, individuals will be able to:

1. Beginning — Design and develop tests for security safeguard performance under normal operating circumstances and workload levels.

2. Intermediate — Design and develop tests for security safeguard performance under abnormal, unusual, improbable, and/or illegal circumstances.

3. Advanced — Ensure that all security-related elements (e.g., system components, documentation) will be effectively tested.

Sample Job Functions —

- IT Security Officer/Manager
- Programmer/Systems Analyst
- System Designer/Developer

INFORMATION TECHNOLOGY SECURITY TRAINING MATRIX — **Cell 3.3C**
Training Area: **System Life Cycle Security — Test & Evaluate** Functional Specialty: **Design & Develop**

IT SECURITY BODY OF KNOWLEDGE TOPICS AND CONCEPTS

- 9 — ACQUISITION/DEVELOPMENT/INSTALLATION/ IMPLEMENTATION CONTROLS

- 10 — OPERATIONAL CONTROLS

- 12 — TECHNICAL CONTROLS

For the content of the numbered topics and concepts above, refer to ***Exhibit 4-4***.

Information Technology Security Training Requirements

INFORMATION TECHNOLOGY SECURITY TRAINING MATRIX — Cell 3.3D

Training Area: **System Life Cycle Security — Test & Evaluate**
Functional Specialty: **Implement & Operate**

Definition — The system life cycle is a model for building and operating an IT system from its initial inception to its termination and disposal of assets. The model includes six phases: Initiation, Development, Test and Evaluation, Implementation, Operations, and Termination. Life cycle security is the ensemble of processes and procedures which ensures data confidentiality, as needed, as well as data and system integrity, and availability.

The test and evaluation phase is the series of steps followed to ensure that the design and construction of a new or modified information system or technology has successfully incorporated appropriate security safeguards.

Behavioral Outcome — Individuals responsible for system implementation or operation are able to conduct tests of the effectiveness of security safeguards in the integrated system.

Knowledge Levels —

1. Beginning — Conduct, Apply, Recognize, Document
2. Intermediate — Assess, Understand, Interpret
3. Advanced — Evaluate, Decide, Recommend

Sample Learning Objectives —

At the conclusion of this module, individuals will be able to:

1. Beginning — Conduct tests of security safeguards in accordance with the established test plan and procedures.

2. Intermediate — Assess the performance of security controls (to include hardware, software, firmware, and telecommunications as appropriate) to ensure that the residual risk is within an acceptable range.

3. Advanced — Evaluate functional operation and performance in light of test results and make recommendations regarding certification and accreditation.

Sample Job Functions —

- Certification Reviewer
- Database Administrator
- Designated Approving Authority
- IT Security Officer/Manager
- Network Administrator
- Programmer/Systems Analyst
- System Administrator
- System Operations Personnel

Information Technology Security Training Requirements

INFORMATION TECHNOLOGY SECURITY TRAINING MATRIX — Cell 3.3D

Training Area: **System Life Cycle Security — Test & Evaluate**
Functional Specialty: **Implement & Operate**

IT SECURITY BODY OF KNOWLEDGE TOPICS AND CONCEPTS

- 3 — SYSTEM ENVIRONMENT
- 4 — SYSTEM INTERCONNECTION
- 5 — INFORMATION SHARING
- 7 — RISK MANAGEMENT
- 8 — MANAGEMENT CONTROLS
- 9 — ACQUISITION/DEVELOPMENT/INSTALLATION/ IMPLEMENTATION CONTROLS
- 10 — OPERATIONAL CONTROLS
- 12 — TECHNICAL CONTROLS

For the content of the numbered topics and concepts above, refer to **Exhibit 4-4**.

Information Technology Security Training Requirements

INFORMATION TECHNOLOGY SECURITY TRAINING MATRIX — **Cell 3.3E**
Training Area: **System Life Cycle Security — Test & Evaluate** Functional Specialty: **Review & Evaluate**

Definition —	The system life cycle is a model for building and operating an IT system from its initial inception to its termination and disposal of assets. The model includes six phases: Initiation, Development, Test and Evaluation, Implementation, Operations, and Termination. Life cycle security is the ensemble of processes and procedures which ensures data confidentiality, as needed, as well as data and system integrity, and availability. The test and evaluation phase is the series of steps followed to ensure that the design and construction of a new or modified information system or technology has successfully incorporated appropriate security safeguards.
Behavioral Outcome —	Individuals are able to evaluate the appropriateness of test methodologies, and conduct independent tests and evaluations to ensure that adequate and appropriate safeguards are in place, effective, and documented; and to prepare certification/accreditation documentation.

Knowledge Levels —

1. Beginning — Know, Perform, Apply
2. Intermediate/Advanced — Evaluate, Interpret, Decide

Sample Learning Objectives —

At the conclusion of this module, individuals will be able to:

1. Beginning — Participate in or perform independent tests and document results.

2. Intermediate/Advanced — Evaluate configuration controls, review security test plans and procedures, ensure that documented security requirements are tested and comply with formal design specifications, and prepare certification/accreditation documentation.

Sample Job Functions —

- Auditor, External
- Auditor, Internal
- Certification Reviewer
- Designated Approving Authority (DAA)
- Information Resources Management (IRM) Official, Senior
- IT Security Officer/Manager
- System Owner

Information Technology Security Training Requirements

INFORMATION TECHNOLOGY SECURITY TRAINING MATRIX — **Cell 3.3E**
Training Area: **System Life Cycle Security — Test & Evaluate** Functional Specialty: **Review & Evaluate**

IT SECURITY BODY OF KNOWLEDGE TOPICS AND CONCEPTS

- 3 — SYSTEM ENVIRONMENT
- 4 — SYSTEM INTERCONNECTION
- 5 — INFORMATION SHARING
- 8 — MANAGEMENT CONTROLS
- 9 — ACQUISITION/DEVELOPMENT/INSTALLATION/ IMPLEMENTATION CONTROLS
- 10 — OPERATIONAL CONTROLS
- 12 — TECHNICAL CONTROLS

For the content of the numbered topics and concepts above, refer to **Exhibit 4-4**.

INFORMATION TECHNOLOGY SECURITY TRAINING MATRIX — Cell 3.3F

Training Area: **System Life Cycle Security — Test & Evaluate**
Functional Specialty: **Use**

Definition — The system life cycle is a model for building and operating an IT system from its initial inception to its termination and disposal of assets. The model includes six phases: Initiation, Development, Test and Evaluation, Implementation, Operations, and Termination. Life cycle security is the ensemble of processes and procedures which ensures data confidentiality, as needed, as well as data and system integrity, and availability.

The test and evaluation phase is the series of steps followed to ensure that the design and construction of a new or modified information system or technology has successfully incorporated appropriate security safeguards.

Behavioral Outcome — Users are able to participate in acceptance tests and evaluate the impact of security safeguards on the operational environment.

Knowledge Levels —

1. Beginning/Intermediate/Advanced — Develop, Evaluate, Decide

Sample Learning Objectives —

At the conclusion of this module, individuals will be able to:

1. Beginning/Intermediate/Advanced — Develop test scenarios for use in acceptance testing of security countermeasures in a normal work environment. Participate in the evaluation of test results to determine the impact of security safeguards on user operations.

Sample Job Functions —

- IT Security Officer/Manager
- System Owner
- User

Information Technology Security Training Requirements

INFORMATION TECHNOLOGY SECURITY TRAINING MATRIX — **Cell 3.3F**

Training Area: **System Life Cycle Security — Test & Evaluate**
Functional Specialty: **Use**

IT SECURITY BODY OF KNOWLEDGE TOPICS AND CONCEPTS

- 8 — MANAGEMENT CONTROLS

- 10 — OPERATIONAL CONTROLS

*For the content of the numbered topics and concepts above, refer to **Exhibit 4-4**.*

INFORMATION TECHNOLOGY SECURITY TRAINING MATRIX — **Cell 3.4A**
Training Area: **System Life Cycle Security — Implementation** Functional Specialty: **Manage**

Definition —	The system life cycle is a model for building and operating an IT system from its initial inception to its termination and disposal of assets. The model includes six phases: Initiation, Development, Test and Evaluation, Implementation, Operations, and Termination. Life cycle security is the ensemble of processes and procedures which ensures data confidentiality, as needed, as well as data and system integrity, and availability. The implementation phase is the installation of the system into the operational environment in a manner that does not compromise the integrity and effectiveness of the successfully tested security safeguards.

Behavioral Outcome — Individuals with management responsibilities are able to oversee the implementation and deployment of an IT system in a manner that does not compromise in-place and tested security safeguards.

Knowledge Levels —

1. Beginning/Intermediate/Advanced — Understand, Ensure, Decide

Sample Learning Objectives —

At the conclusion of this module, individuals will be able to:

1. Beginning/Intermediate/Advanced — Decide whether to continue system deployment if unanticipated circumstances are encountered that compromise security safeguards. Ensure that final implementation in the production environment does not compromise security safeguards.

Sample Job Functions —

- Information Resources Management (IRM) Official, Senior
- Information Resources Manager
- IT Security Officer/Manager
- Program Manager
- System Owner

INFORMATION TECHNOLOGY SECURITY TRAINING MATRIX — Cell 3.4A

Training Area: **System Life Cycle Security — Implementation**
Functional Specialty: **Manage**

IT SECURITY BODY OF KNOWLEDGE TOPICS AND CONCEPTS

- 3 — SYSTEM ENVIRONMENT
- 4 — SYSTEM INTERCONNECTION
- 5 — INFORMATION SHARING
- 8 — MANAGEMENT CONTROLS
- 9 — ACQUISITION/DEVELOPMENT/INSTALLATION/ IMPLEMENTATION CONTROLS
- 10 — OPERATIONAL CONTROLS
- 12 — TECHNICAL CONTROLS

*For the content of the numbered topics and concepts above, refer to **Exhibit 4-4**.*

INFORMATION TECHNOLOGY SECURITY TRAINING MATRIX — Cell 3.4B

Training Area: System Life Cycle Security — Implementation
Functional Specialty: Acquire

Definition — The system life cycle is a model for building and operating an IT system from its initial inception to its termination and disposal of assets. The model includes six phases: Initiation, Development, Test and Evaluation, Implementation, Operations, and Termination. Life cycle security is the ensemble of processes and procedures which ensures data confidentiality, as needed, as well as data and system integrity, and availability.

The implementation phase is the installation of the system into the operational environment in a manner that does not compromise the integrity and effectiveness of the successfully tested security safeguards.

Behavioral Outcome — Individuals with acquisition responsibilities are able to ensure that the system, as implemented, meets all contractual requirements related to the security and privacy of IT resources.

Knowledge Levels —

1. Beginning/Intermediate — Know, Review, Decide
2. Advanced — Determine, Interpret, Authorize

Sample Learning Objectives —

At the conclusion of this module, individuals will be able to:

1. Beginning/Intermediate — Monitor contract performance and review deliverables for conformance with contract requirements related to IT security and privacy.

2. Advanced — Take action as needed to ensure that accepted products meet contract requirements.

Sample Job Functions —

- Contracting Officer
- Contracting Officer's Technical Representative (COTR)
- IT Security Officer/Manager
- Program Manager
- System Owner

Information Technology Security Training Requirements

INFORMATION TECHNOLOGY SECURITY TRAINING MATRIX — Cell 3.4B

Training Area: **System Life Cycle Security — Implementation**
Functional Specialty: **Acquire**

IT SECURITY BODY OF KNOWLEDGE TOPICS AND CONCEPTS

- 9 — ACQUISITION/DEVELOPMENT/INSTALLATION/ IMPLEMENTATION CONTROLS

- 10 — OPERATIONAL CONTROLS

- 12 — TECHNICAL CONTROLS

For the content of the numbered topics and concepts above, refer to ***Exhibit 4-4****.*

INFORMATION TECHNOLOGY SECURITY TRAINING MATRIX — Cell 3.4C

Training Area: **System Life Cycle Security — Implementation**
Functional Specialty: **Design & Develop**

Definition — The system life cycle is a model for building and operating an IT system from its initial inception to its termination and disposal of assets. The model includes six phases: Initiation, Development, Test and Evaluation, Implementation, Operations, and Termination. Life cycle security is the ensemble of processes and procedures which ensures data confidentiality, as needed, as well as data and system integrity, and availability.

The implementation phase is the installation of the system into the operational environment in a manner that does not compromise the integrity and effectiveness of the successfully tested security safeguards.

Behavioral Outcome — Individuals responsible for system design and/or modification are able to participate in the development of procedures which ensure that safeguards are not compromised as they are incorporated into the production environment.

Knowledge Levels —

1. Beginning — Know, Understand, Identify
2. Intermediate — Interpret, Assess, Apply
3. Advanced — Determine, Recommend, Select

Sample Learning Objectives —

At the conclusion of this module, individuals will be able to:

1. Beginning — Identify IT security impacts associated with system implementation procedures.

2. Intermediate — Participate in the design, development, and modification of safeguards to correct vulnerabilities identified during system implementation.

3. Advanced — Lead the design, development, and modification of safeguards to correct vulnerabilities identified during system implementation.

Sample Job Functions —

- Database Administrator
- IT Security Officer/Manager
- Network Administrator
- Program Manager
- Programmer/Systems Analyst
- System Administrator
- System Designer/Developer
- Systems Operations Personnel

INFORMATION TECHNOLOGY SECURITY TRAINING MATRIX — **Cell 3.4C**
Training Area: **System Life Cycle Security — Implementation** Functional Specialty: **Design & Develop**

IT SECURITY BODY OF KNOWLEDGE TOPICS AND CONCEPTS

- 3 — SYSTEM ENVIRONMENT
- 4 — SYSTEM INTERCONNECTION
- 5 — INFORMATION SHARING
- 8 — MANAGEMENT CONTROLS
- 9 — ACQUISITION/DEVELOPMENT/INSTALLATION/ IMPLEMENTATION CONTROLS
- 10 — OPERATIONAL CONTROLS
- 12 — TECHNICAL CONTROLS

For the content of the numbered topics and concepts above, refer to ***Exhibit 4-4***.

Information Technology Security Training Requirements

INFORMATION TECHNOLOGY SECURITY TRAINING MATRIX — **Cell 3.4D**
Training Area: **System Life Cycle Security — Implementation**   Functional Specialty: **Implement & Operate**

Definition — The system life cycle is a model for building and operating an IT system from its initial inception to its termination and disposal of assets. The model includes six phases: Initiation, Development, Test and Evaluation, Implementation, Operations, and Termination. Life cycle security is the ensemble of processes and procedures which ensures data confidentiality, as needed, as well as data and system integrity, and availability.

The implementation phase is the installation of the system into the operational environment in a manner that does not compromise the integrity and effectiveness of the successfully tested security safeguards.

Behavioral Outcome — Individuals responsible for system implementation or operation ensure that approved safeguards are in place and effective as the system moves into production.

Knowledge Levels —

1. Beginning — Know, Apply, Recognize
2. Intermediate — Identify, Interpret, Decide
3. Advanced — Analyze, Determine, Approve

Sample Learning Objectives —

At the conclusion of this module, individuals will be able to:

1. Beginning — Participate in the implementation of safeguards for an IT system in accordance with the established implementation plan.

2. Intermediate — Identify vulnerabilities resulting from a departure from the implementation plan or that were not apparent during testing. Determine necessary actions to return the implementation process to the established plan or to forward identified vulnerabilities for resolution.

3. Advanced — Examine unresolved system vulnerabilities and determine what corrective action or additional safeguards are necessary to mitigate them.

Sample Job Functions —

- Database Administrator
- IT Security Officer/Manager
- Network Administrator
- System Administrator
- Systems Operations Personnel
- Technical Support Personnel

Chapter 4. Training Development Methodology

INFORMATION TECHNOLOGY SECURITY TRAINING MATRIX — Cell 3.4D

Training Area: **System Life Cycle Security — Implementation**
Functional Specialty: **Implement & Operate**

IT SECURITY BODY OF KNOWLEDGE TOPICS AND CONCEPTS

- 3 — SYSTEM ENVIRONMENT
- 4 — SYSTEM INTERCONNECTION
- 5 — INFORMATION SHARING
- 9 — ACQUISITION/DEVELOPMENT/INSTALLATION/IMPLEMENTATION CONTROLS
- 10 — OPERATIONAL CONTROLS
- 12 — TECHNICAL CONTROLS

For the content of the numbered topics and concepts above, refer to **Exhibit 4-4**.

INFORMATION TECHNOLOGY SECURITY TRAINING MATRIX — Cell 3.4E

Training Area: System Life Cycle Security — Implementation
Functional Specialty: Review & Evaluate

Definition — The system life cycle is a model for building and operating an IT system from its initial inception to its termination and disposal of assets. The model includes six phases: Initiation, Development, Test and Evaluation, Implementation, Operations, and Termination. Life cycle security is the ensemble of processes and procedures which ensures data confidentiality, as needed, as well as data and system integrity, and availability.

The implementation phase is the installation of the system into the operational environment in a manner that does not compromise the integrity and effectiveness of the successfully tested security safeguards.

Behavioral Outcome — Individuals responsible for review and evaluation are able to analyze system and test documentation to determine whether the system provides adequate and appropriate IT security to support certification and accreditation.

Knowledge Levels —

1. Beginning/Intermediate — Understand, Review, Evaluate
2. Advanced — Analyze, Decide, Recommend

Sample Learning Objectives —

At the conclusion of this module, individuals will be able to:

1. Beginning/Intermediate — Review and evaluate the effectiveness of safeguards, the maintainability of IT security features, the adequacy of system documentation, and the efficiency of system security administration.

2. Advanced — Recommend IT system certification/accreditation and/or measures required to achieve/maintain approval to operate.

Sample Job Functions —

- Auditor, External
- Auditor, Internal
- Certification Reviewer
- Chief Information Officer
- Designated Approving Authority (DAA)
- IT Security Officer/Manager
- Program Manager
- System Owner

INFORMATION TECHNOLOGY SECURITY TRAINING MATRIX — **Cell 3.4E**
Training Area: **System Life Cycle Security — Implementation** Functional Specialty: **Review & Evaluate**

IT SECURITY BODY OF KNOWLEDGE TOPICS AND CONCEPTS

- 3 — SYSTEM ENVIRONMENT
- 4 — SYSTEM INTERCONNECTION
- 6 — SENSITIVITY
- 8 — MANAGEMENT CONTROLS
- 9 — ACQUISITION/DEVELOPMENT/INSTALLATION/ IMPLEMENTATION CONTROLS
- 10 — OPERATIONAL CONTROLS
- 12 — TECHNICAL CONTROLS

*For the content of the numbered topics and concepts above, refer to **Exhibit 4-4**.*

Information Technology Security Training Requirements

INFORMATION TECHNOLOGY SECURITY TRAINING MATRIX — Cell 3.4F

Training Area: **System Life Cycle Security — Implementation**
Functional Specialty: **Use**

Definition — The system life cycle is a model for building and operating an IT system from its initial inception to its termination and disposal of assets. The model includes six phases: Initiation, Development, Test and Evaluation, Implementation, Operations, and Termination. Life cycle security is the ensemble of processes and procedures which ensures data confidentiality, as needed, as well as data and system integrity, and availability.

The implementation phase is the installation of the system into the operational environment in a manner that does not compromise the integrity and effectiveness of the successfully tested security safeguards.

Behavioral Outcome — Users are able to identify and report security and efficiency concerns encountered during normal operations.

Knowledge Levels —

1. Beginning/Intermediate/Advanced — Know, Apply, Identify

Sample Learning Objectives —

At the conclusion of this module, individuals will be able to:

1. Beginning/Intermediate/Advanced — Follow procedures for using the IT system in a secure manner; identify and report potential security events and efficiency concerns.

Sample Job Functions —

- IT Security Officer/Manager
- User

INFORMATION TECHNOLOGY SECURITY TRAINING MATRIX — Cell 3.4F

Training Area: **System Life Cycle Security — Implementation**
Functional Specialty: **Use**

IT SECURITY BODY OF KNOWLEDGE TOPICS AND CONCEPTS

- 6 — SENSITIVITY

- 8 — MANAGEMENT CONTROLS

For the content of the numbered topics and concepts above, refer to ***Exhibit 4-4***.

Information Technology Security Training Requirements

INFORMATION TECHNOLOGY SECURITY TRAINING MATRIX — **Cell 3.5A**
Training Area: **System Life Cycle Security — Operations** Functional Specialty: **Manage**

Definition —	The system life cycle is a model for building and operating an IT system from its initial inception to its termination and disposal of assets. The model includes six phases: Initiation, Development, Test and Evaluation, Implementation, Operations, and Termination. Life cycle security is the ensemble of processes and procedures which ensures data confidentiality, as needed, as well as data and system integrity, and availability. The operations phase includes the ongoing day-to-day use (production) and maintenance or enhancement of the system without compromising the integrity and effectiveness of the installed safeguards.

Behavioral Outcome —	Individuals with management responsibilities are able to monitor operations to ensure that safeguards are effective and have the intended effect of balancing efficiency with minimized risk.

Knowledge Levels —

1. Beginning — Know, Understand, Decide
2. Intermediate — Direct, Provide, Identify
3. Advanced — Monitor, Evaluate, Select

Sample Learning Objectives —

At the conclusion of this module, individuals will be able to:

1. Beginning — Understand the in-place IT security procedures and safeguards and the assignment of responsibilities to ensure that operations personnel are complying with them.

2. Intermediate — Provide leadership and direction to operations personnel by ensuring that IT security awareness, basics and literacy, and training are provided to operations personnel commensurate with their responsibilities.

3. Advanced — Monitor and evaluate the effectiveness of IT security procedures and safeguards to ensure they provide the intended level of protection. Take action as necessary should the level of protection fall below the established minimum.

Sample Job Functions —

- Data Center Manager
- IT Security Officer/Manager
- Network Administrator
- Program Manager
- System Administrator
- System Owner

Chapter 4. Training Development Methodology

INFORMATION TECHNOLOGY SECURITY TRAINING MATRIX — **Cell 3.5A**
Training Area: **System Life Cycle Security — Operations** Functional Specialty: **Manage**

IT SECURITY BODY OF KNOWLEDGE TOPICS AND CONCEPTS

- 4 — SYSTEM INTERCONNECTION
- 5 — INFORMATION SHARING
- 8 — MANAGEMENT CONTROLS
- 9 — ACQUISITION/DEVELOPMENT/INSTALLATION/ IMPLEMENTATION CONTROLS
- 10 — OPERATIONAL CONTROLS
- 11 — AWARENESS, TRAINING, AND EDUCATION CONTROLS
- 12 — TECHNICAL CONTROLS

For the content of the numbered topics and concepts above, refer to **Exhibit 4-4**.

INFORMATION TECHNOLOGY SECURITY TRAINING MATRIX — **Cell 3.5B**
Training Area: **System Life Cycle Security — Operations** Functional Specialty: **Acquire**
Definition — The system life cycle is a model for building and operating an IT system from its initial inception to its termination and disposal of assets. The model includes six phases: Initiation, Development, Test and Evaluation, Implementation, Operations, and Termination. Life cycle security is the ensemble of processes and procedures which ensures data confidentiality, as needed, as well as data and system integrity, and availability. The operations phase includes the ongoing day-to-day use (production) and maintenance or enhancement of the system without compromising the integrity and effectiveness of the installed safeguards.
Behavioral Outcome — Individuals with acquisition responsibilities are able to understand the IT security concerns associated with system operations and to identify and use the appropriate contract vehicle to meet current needs in a timely manner.
Knowledge Levels — 1. Beginning/Intermediate — Know, Review, Decide 2. Advanced — Determine, Interpret, Authorize
Sample Learning Objectives — At the conclusion of this module, individuals will be able to: 1. Beginning/Intermediate — Monitor contract performance and review deliverables for conformance with contract requirements related to IT security and privacy. 2. Advanced — Take action as needed to ensure that accepted products/services meet contract requirements.
Sample Job Functions — • Contracting Officer • Contracting Officer's Technical Representative (COTR) • IT Security Officer/Manager • Program Manager • System Owner

INFORMATION TECHNOLOGY SECURITY TRAINING MATRIX — **Cell 3.5B**

Training Area: **System Life Cycle Security — Operations**
Functional Specialty: **Acquire**

IT SECURITY BODY OF KNOWLEDGE TOPICS AND CONCEPTS

- 8 — MANAGEMENT CONTROLS

- 9 — ACQUISITION/DEVELOPMENT/INSTALLATION/ IMPLEMENTATION CONTROLS

- 10 — OPERATIONAL CONTROLS

- 12 — TECHNICAL CONTROLS

For the content of the numbered topics and concepts above, refer to **Exhibit 4-4**.

INFORMATION TECHNOLOGY SECURITY TRAINING MATRIX — Cell 3.5C

Training Area: **System Life Cycle Security — Operations**
Functional Specialty: **Design & Develop**

Definition — The system life cycle is a model for building and operating an IT system from its initial inception to its termination and disposal of assets. The model includes six phases: Initiation, Development, Test and Evaluation, Implementation, Operations, and Termination. Life cycle security is the ensemble of processes and procedures which ensures data confidentiality, as needed, as well as data and system integrity, and availability.

The operations phase includes the ongoing day-to-day use (production) and maintenance or enhancement of the system without compromising the integrity and effectiveness of the installed safeguards.

Behavioral Outcome — Individuals responsible for system development are able to make procedural and operational changes necessary to maintain the acceptable level of risk.

Knowledge Levels —

1. Beginning/Intermediate — Develop, Know, Understand
2. Advanced — Select, Analyze, Decide

Sample Learning Objectives —

At the conclusion of this module, individuals will be able to:

1. Beginning/Intermediate — Design/develop new or modified IT security procedures or safeguards to accommodate changes in operations.

2. Advanced — Modify/select IT security procedures/safeguards that enhance the existing level of security and integrity.

Sample Job Functions —

- IT Security Officer/Manager
- Network Administrator
- Programmer/Systems Analyst
- System Administrator
- System Designer/Developer
- Systems Operations Personnel

Information Technology Security Training Requirements

INFORMATION TECHNOLOGY SECURITY TRAINING MATRIX — **Cell 3.5C**

Training Area: **System Life Cycle Security — Operations**
Functional Specialty: **Design & Develop**

IT SECURITY BODY OF KNOWLEDGE TOPICS AND CONCEPTS

- 3 — SYSTEM ENVIRONMENT

- 4 — SYSTEM INTERCONNECTION

- 5 — INFORMATION SHARING

- 7 — RISK MANAGEMENT

- 9 — ACQUISITION/DEVELOPMENT/INSTALLATION/ IMPLEMENTATION CONTROLS

*For the content of the numbered topics and concepts above, refer to **Exhibit 4-4**.*

INFORMATION TECHNOLOGY SECURITY TRAINING MATRIX — Cell 3.5D

Training Area: System Life Cycle Security — Operations
Functional Specialty: Implement & Operate

Definition — The system life cycle is a model for building and operating an IT system from its initial inception to its termination and disposal of assets. The model includes six phases: Initiation, Development, Test and Evaluation, Implementation, Operations, and Termination. Life cycle security is the ensemble of processes and procedures which ensures data confidentiality, as needed, as well as data and system integrity, and availability.

The operations phase includes the ongoing day-to-day use (production) and maintenance or enhancement of the system without compromising the integrity and effectiveness of the installed safeguards.

Behavioral Outcome — Individuals responsible for system implementation or operation are able to maintain appropriate safeguards continuously within acceptable levels of risk.

Knowledge Levels —

1. Beginning — Know, Participate, Monitor
2. Intermediate — Evaluate, Identify, Execute
3. Advanced — Analyze, Interpret, Recommend

Sample Learning Objectives —

At the conclusion of this module, individuals will be able to:

1. Beginning — Participate in maintaining safeguards in accordance with standard operating procedures. Monitor system activity to identify potential IT security events.

2. Intermediate — Evaluate potential It security events, identify actual security incidents, and take appropriate corrective and recovery actions.

3. Advanced — Analyze IT security incidents or patterns of incidents to determine if remedial actions are needed to correct vulnerabilities and maintain the acceptable level of risk.

Sample Job Functions —

- Database Administrator
- IT Security Officer/Manager
- Network Administrator
- System Administrator
- System Operations Personnel
- Technical Support Personnel
- Telecommunications Specialist

Information Technology Security Training Requirements

INFORMATION TECHNOLOGY SECURITY TRAINING MATRIX — Cell 3.5D

Training Area: System Life Cycle Security — Operations
Functional Specialty: Implement & Operate

IT SECURITY BODY OF KNOWLEDGE TOPICS AND CONCEPTS

- 7 — RISK MANAGEMENT

- 8 — MANAGEMENT CONTROLS

- 9 — ACQUISITION/DEVELOPMENT/INSTALLATION/ IMPLEMENTATION CONTROLS

- 10 — OPERATIONAL CONTROLS

- 11 — AWARENESS, TRAINING, AND EDUCATION CONTROLS

- 12 — TECHNICAL CONTROLS

For the content of the numbered topics and concepts above, refer to **Exhibit 4-4**.

INFORMATION TECHNOLOGY SECURITY TRAINING MATRIX — Cell 3.5E

Training Area: **System Life Cycle Security — Operations**
Functional Specialty: **Review & Evaluate**

Definition — The system life cycle is a model for building and operating an IT system from its initial inception to its termination and disposal of assets. The model includes six phases: Initiation, Development, Test and Evaluation, Implementation, Operations, and Termination. Life cycle security is the ensemble of processes and procedures which ensures data confidentiality, as needed, as well as data and system integrity, and availability.

The operations phase includes the ongoing day-to-day use (production) and maintenance or enhancement of the system without compromising the integrity and effectiveness of the installed safeguards.

Behavioral Outcome — Individuals responsible for review and evaluation are able to examine the operational system to determine the adequacy and effectiveness of safeguards and to ensure that a consistent and appropriate level of security (i.e., one with an acceptable level of risk) is maintained.

Knowledge Levels —

1. Beginning — Understand, Participate, Identify
2. Intermediate — Analyze, Determine, Apply
3. Advanced — Decide, Recommend, Interpret

Sample Learning Objectives —

At the conclusion of this module, individuals will be able to:

1. Beginning — Participate in the evaluation of an operational system to determine the adequacy and effectiveness of security safeguards and environment, leading to continued approval to operate (recertification and re-accreditation).

2. Intermediate — Determine the adequacy of security environments and the capability of security strategies, architectures, and safeguards to maintain the integrity of those security environments. Prepare recommendations for system approval decisions.

3. Advanced — Recommend IT system recertification/re-accreditation and/or corrective actions required to achieve/maintain certification/accreditation.

Sample Job Functions —

- Auditor, External
- Auditor, Internal
- Certification Reviewer
- Designated Approving Authority (DAA)
- IT Security Officer/Manager

Information Technology Security Training Requirements

INFORMATION TECHNOLOGY SECURITY TRAINING MATRIX — Cell 3.5E

Training Area: **System Life Cycle Security — Operations**
Functional Specialty: **Review & Evaluate**

IT SECURITY BODY OF KNOWLEDGE TOPICS AND CONCEPTS

- 7 — RISK MANAGEMENT

- 9 — ACQUISITION/DEVELOPMENT/INSTALLATION/ IMPLEMENTATION CONTROLS

- 10 — OPERATIONAL CONTROLS

- 11 — AWARENESS, TRAINING, AND EDUCATION CONTROLS

- 12 — TECHNICAL CONTROLS

For the content of the numbered topics and concepts above, refer to ***Exhibit 4-4****.*

INFORMATION TECHNOLOGY SECURITY TRAINING MATRIX — Cell 3.5F	
Training Area: **System Life Cycle Security — Operations** Functional Specialty: **Use**	
Definition —	The system life cycle is a model for building and operating an IT system from its initial inception to its termination and disposal of assets. The model includes six phases: Initiation, Development, Test and Evaluation, Implementation, Operations, and Termination. Life cycle security is the ensemble of processes and procedures which ensures data confidentiality, as needed, as well as data and system integrity, and availability. The operations phase includes the ongoing day-to-day use (production) and maintenance or enhancement of the system without compromising the integrity and effectiveness of the installed safeguards.
Behavioral Outcome — Users are able to understand the objectives of and comply with the "rules of behavior" for the system.	
Knowledge Levels — 1. Beginning/Intermediate/Advanced — Know, Identify, Apply	
Sample Learning Objectives — At the conclusion of this module, individuals will be able to: 1. Beginning/Intermediate/Advanced — Follow procedures for using the IT system in a secure manner; identify and report potential security events.	
Sample Job Functions — • IT Security Officer/Manager • User	

INFORMATION TECHNOLOGY SECURITY TRAINING MATRIX — Cell 3.5F

Training Area: System Life Cycle Security — Operations
Functional Specialty: Use

IT SECURITY BODY OF KNOWLEDGE TOPICS AND CONCEPTS

- 8 — MANAGEMENT CONTROLS

- 10 — OPERATIONAL CONTROLS

- 12 — TECHNICAL CONTROLS

For the content of the numbered topics and concepts above, refer to ***Exhibit 4-4****.*

INFORMATION TECHNOLOGY SECURITY TRAINING MATRIX — Cell 3.6A

Training Area: **System Life Cycle Security — Termination**
Functional Specialty: **Manage**

Definition —	The system life cycle is a model for building and operating an IT system from its initial inception to its termination and disposal of assets. The model includes six phases: Initiation, Development, Test and Evaluation, Implementation, Operations, and Termination. Life cycle security is the ensemble of processes and procedures which ensures data confidentiality, as needed, as well as data and system integrity, and availability. The termination phase comprises the series of steps taken to retire a system when it is no longer needed and to securely and properly archive or dispose of its assets.
Behavioral Outcome —	Individuals with management responsibilities are able to understand the special IT security considerations and measures required during the shutdown of a system, and effectively plan and direct these activities.

Knowledge Levels —

1. Beginning — Understand, Apply, Monitor
2. Intermediate/Advanced — Validate, Decide, Direct, Approve

Sample Learning Objectives —

At the conclusion of this module, individuals will be able to:

1. Beginning — Understand and ensure compliance with the IT security considerations and procedures required for termination of the system.

2. Intermediate/Advanced — Ensure that appropriate and adequate plans and procedures are established, validate the termination plan, and accept the residual level of risk.

Sample Job Functions —

- Database Administrator
- Data Center Manager
- IT Security Officer/Manager
- Program Manager
- System Owner

INFORMATION TECHNOLOGY SECURITY TRAINING MATRIX — Cell 3.6A

Training Area: **System Life Cycle Security —Termination**
Functional Specialty: **Manage**

IT SECURITY BODY OF KNOWLEDGE TOPICS AND CONCEPTS

- 1 — LAWS AND REGULATIONS

- 5 — INFORMATION SHARING

- 6 — SENSITIVITY

- 7 — RISK MANAGEMENT

*For the content of the numbered topics and concepts above, refer to **Exhibit 4-4**.*

Information Technology Security Training Requirements

INFORMATION TECHNOLOGY SECURITY TRAINING MATRIX — **Cell 3.6D**
Training Area: **System Life Cycle Security — Termination** Functional Specialty: **Implement & Operate**
Definition — The system life cycle is a model for building and operating an IT system from its initial inception to its termination and disposal of assets. The model includes six phases: Initiation, Development, Test and Evaluation, Implementation, Operations, and Termination. Life cycle security is the ensemble of processes and procedures which ensures data confidentiality, as needed, as well as data and system integrity, and availability. The termination phase comprises the series of steps taken to retire a system when it is no longer needed and to securely and properly archive or dispose of its assets.
Behavioral Outcome — Individuals responsible for IT system operation are able to develop and implement the system termination plan, including security requirements for archiving/disposing of resources.
Knowledge Levels — 1. Beginning — Understand, Comply, Report 2. Intermediate — Apply, Decide, Conduct 3. Advanced — Analyze, Determine, Develop **Sample Learning Objectives** — At the conclusion of this module, individuals will be able to: 1. Beginning — Comply with termination procedures and report any potential IT security incidents or actual breaches to proper authorities. 2. Intermediate — Ensure that hardware, software, data, and facility resources are archived, sanitized, or disposed of in a manner consistent with the system termination plan. 3. Advanced — Develop the system termination plan to ensure that IT security breaches are avoided during shutdown and long-term protection of archived resources is achieved.
Sample Job Functions — - Contracting Officer's Technical Representative - Data Center Manager - Database Administrator - FOIA Official - IT Security Officer/Manager - Network Administrator - Privacy Act Official - Program Manager - Programmer/Systems Analyst - Records Management Official - System Administrator - Systems Operations Personnel - Technical Support Personnel

Information Technology Security Training Requirements

INFORMATION TECHNOLOGY SECURITY TRAINING MATRIX — **Cell 3.6D**
Training Area: **System Life Cycle Security —Termination** Functional Specialty: **Implement & Operate**

IT SECURITY BODY OF KNOWLEDGE TOPICS AND CONCEPTS

- 5 — INFORMATION SHARING

- 6 — SENSITIVITY

- 7 — RISK MANAGEMENT

For the content of the numbered topics and concepts above, refer to ***Exhibit 4-4***.

Information Technology Security Training Requirements

INFORMATION TECHNOLOGY SECURITY TRAINING MATRIX — **Cell 3.6E**
Training Area: **System Life Cycle Security — Termination** Functional Specialty: **Review & Evaluate**
Definition — The system life cycle is a model for building and operating an IT system from its initial inception to its termination and disposal of assets. The model includes six phases: Initiation, Development, Test and Evaluation, Implementation, Operations, and Termination. Life cycle security is the ensemble of processes and procedures which ensures data confidentiality, as needed, as well as data and system integrity, and availability. The termination phase comprises the series of steps taken to retire a system when it is no longer needed and to securely and properly archive or dispose of its assets.
Behavioral Outcome — Individuals responsible for review and evaluation are able to verify the appropriateness of the termination plan and processes used to terminate the IT system securely.
Knowledge Levels — 1. Beginning/Intermediate/Advanced — Evaluate, Determine, Verify
Sample Learning Objectives — At the conclusion of this module, individuals will be able to: 1. Beginning/Intermediate/Advanced — Evaluate the termination plan and procedures to ensure that IT security and archival concerns have been appropriately addressed.
Sample Job Functions — - Auditor, External - Auditor, Internal - Information Resources Manager - IT Security Officer/Manager - Records Management Official

Chapter 4. Training Development Methodology

Information Technology Security Training Requirements

INFORMATION TECHNOLOGY SECURITY TRAINING MATRIX — Cell 3.6E

Training Area: **System Life Cycle Security —Termination**
Functional Specialty: **Review & Evaluate**

IT SECURITY BODY OF KNOWLEDGE TOPICS AND CONCEPTS

- 1 — LAWS AND REGULATIONS
- 5 — INFORMATION SHARING
- 6 — SENSITIVITY
- 7 — RISK MANAGEMENT

*For the content of the numbered topics and concepts above, refer to **Exhibit 4-4**.*

Chapter 4. Training Development Methodology

CHAPTER

5

EVALUATING TRAINING EFFECTIVENESS

CHAPTER 5. EVALUATING TRAINING EFFECTIVENESS

Evaluate: "To determine or fix the value of; to examine carefully"[3]

5.1 Value of Evaluation in a Training Program

Evaluating training effectiveness is a vital step to ensure that the training delivered is meaningful. Training is "meaningful" *only* when it meets the needs of both the student (employee) and the organization. If training content is incorrect, outdated, or inappropriate for the audience, the training will not meet student or organizational needs. If the delivery vehicle (e.g., classroom or computer-based training) is inappropriate, either in relation to the simplicity/complexity of the content or to the type of audience—or if there is an inadequate mix of vehicles in an agency's overall training program—the training will not meet needs. Spending time and resources on training that does not achieve desired effects can reinforce, rather than dispel, the perception of security as an obstacle to productivity. Further, it can require the expenditure of far more resources in data or system recovery after a security incident occurs than would have been spent in prevention activities.

All meaningless training is expensive, even where the direct cost outlay, or cost-per-student, may be low. Because agencies cannot afford to waste limited resources on ineffective training, evaluation of training effectiveness should become an integral component of an agency's IT security training program. A robust training evaluation effort may be the second most effective vehicle for garnering management support for IT security—the first being the occurrence of a serious security incident.

In broader context, attention to IT security training evaluation is in line with a changing focus in the overall field of information technology regarding how results of systems efforts are measured. The focus is beginning to change from being solely a machine view, i.e., measuring the functionality of the technology (e.g., speed, gigabytes), to encompass a people view, i.e., the functionality of the people who use the technology. Thus, in organizations where it is recognized that system utility is affected—or even determined—by users, it becomes apparent that to achieve its full utility, a percentage of the system budget must be devoted to people needs such as training.[4]

---

[3] From WEBSTER's II *New Riverside University Dictionary*, Riverside Publishing Company, 1988.

[4] A paraphrase of Ruth's Rule from "User-Centered Evaluation of Information Technology: A Non-Accountant's View of a Significant Opportunity" by Stephen R. Ruth, Ph.D., <u>Government Accountants' Journal</u>, Summer 1996, Vol. 45, No. 2, pp.12-19.

5.2 Purposes of Training Effectiveness Evaluation

Meaningfulness, or effectiveness, requires measurement. Evaluating training effectiveness has four distinct but interrelated purposes—to measure:

- The extent to which conditions were right for learning and the learner's subjective satisfaction;

- What a given student has learned from a specific course or training event, i.e., learning effectiveness;

- A pattern of student outcomes following a specific course or training event; i.e., teaching effectiveness; and

- The value of the specific class or training event, compared to other options in the context of an agency's overall IT security training program; i.e., program effectiveness.

An evaluation process should produce four types of measurement, each related to one of evaluation's four purposes, as appropriate for three types of users of evaluation data:

- First, evaluation should yield information to assist the employees themselves in assessing their subsequent on-the-job performance.

- Second, evaluation should yield information to assist the employees' supervisors in assessing individual students' subsequent on-the-job performance.

- Third, it should produce trend data to assist trainers in improving both learning and teaching.

- Finally, it should produce return-on-investment statistics to enable responsible officials to allocate limited resources in a thoughtful, strategic manner among the spectrum of IT security awareness, security literacy, training, and education options for optimal results among the workforce as a whole.

5.3 Development of an Evaluation Plan

It is difficult to get "good" information for each of evaluation's four purposes (above). It is impossible to do so without planning for evaluation. To evaluate student learning, it is first necessary to have written learning objectives, stated in an observable, measurable way as behavioral outcomes: in short, "behavioral objectives." To evaluate teaching, it is necessary to plan for the collection of trend data, evaluation, and extrapolation. To evaluate return on investment, mission-related goals must be explicitly identified to which the learning objectives are related. *Thus, to obtain "good" information in each of these areas, the process of course development should include the development of an evaluation plan.* The remainder of this section provides guidance in the development of an evaluation plan.

5.3.1 Behavioral Objectives

The major components of behavioral objectives are: Conditions of Activity, Activity to be Performed, and Level of Success. There are several "schools" of behavioral objectives among educational theorists; however, most agree with the three components, described below.

- Conditions of Activity

    This is a written description of existing conditions prior to, and in preparation for, the learning activity. A "snowstorm" metaphor is illustrative. For meteorologists to forecast the arrival of a snowstorm, certain conditions must exist: e.g., relative humidity at a certain level, air temperature, conducive atmospheric conditions. Similarly, certain conditions must be present to forecast training effectiveness. Does the student need a checklist, a set of items to manipulate, or an outline of the information? Does the instructor need audiovisual equipment, handouts, or a classroom with furniture set up in a specific format? Conditions of the learning activity, including computer-based training (CBT), not just "platform" training, must be specific and comprehensive. Keep in mind that if just one of the conditions for a snowstorm is missing, the storm either will not arrive or its force will be diminished. So, too, with learning.

- Activity to be Performed

    The evaluation plan must state the activity to be performed in a manner permitting the evaluator to actually observe the behavior that the student is to learn—whether observable in class (teacher as evaluator) or back on the job (supervisor as evaluator). It is difficult, if not impossible, to measure the process of a student changing an attitude or thinking through a task or problem. The evaluator, however, can measure a written exercise, a skill demonstration, a verbal or written pronouncement, or any combination of these outwardly demonstrable activities. He/she cannot take the student's word for the learned skill, or the simple fact that the student was present and exposed to the skill or information being taught. Rather, the evaluator must observe the skill being performed or the information being applied. (With CBT, evaluation measurement can be programmed to occur at the instructional block level, with subsequent blocks adjusted based on student response. With platform training, adjustments can be made in real time by the instructor based on the nature of student questions during the course. Adjustments can also be made between courses in a student's training sequence.)

- Level of Success

    Measures of success should be derived from the individual's normal work products rather than from classroom testing. This directly ties the individual's performance to its impact on the organization's mission. Written behavioral objectives for a learning activity must include a stated level of success. For quantitative skills, must the learner perform successfully every time, or 10 out of 100 times, or 5 out of 10 times in terms of performance requirements or consequences? Risk management requirements should be used to establish the criticality of quantitative skills. For qualitative skills, what distinguishes satisfactory performance from failure, or outstanding performance from satisfactory? Measurements of qualitative skills might include the amount of re-work required, customer satisfaction, or peer recognition of the employee as a source of IT security information.

    The nature and purpose of the training activity, and whether it is at a beginning, intermediate, or advanced level, will influence the setting of success measures—a subjective goal. If success levels are not documented, an individual student's achievement of the behavioral objectives of the learning activity can not be evaluated, nor can the learning activity itself be evaluated within an organization's overall training program.

In addition to the written objectives suggested above, the evaluation plan should show how the data to be collected are to be used to support the cost and effort of the data collection. This can be related to levels of evaluation, presented below.

5.3.2 Levels of Evaluation

Four levels of evaluation, in order of complexity, are:

- Level 1: End-of-Course Evaluations (Student Satisfaction)

- Level 2: Behavior Objective Testing (Learning Effectiveness, which is also a measure of Teaching Effectiveness)

- Level 3: Job Transfer Skills (Performance Effectiveness)

- Level 4: Organizational Benefit (Training Program Effectiveness)

Altogether, the four levels match the four purposes of training evaluation (described in Section 5.2) in a staged manner. These levels are as follows.

Level 1: End-of-Course Evaluations (Student Satisfaction)

A common term for this type of evaluation is "the 'Smiley Face' evaluation." Likert Scale-type forms ask the student to check a range of options from "poor" to "excellent" (or *vice versa*) to indicate how he/she felt about the class, the computer-based courseware, or whatever the learning activity was. The response data is an indicator of how the learning activity is received by the student. The responses also reveal if the conditions for learning were correct. Some of the questions in this level of evaluation ask about the student's satisfaction with the training facility and instructor (if classroom training), the manner of presentation of the content, and whether or not course objectives were met in relation to the student's expectations. Although this type of evaluation does not provide in-depth data, it does provide rapid feedback from the learner's perspective.

Measurement of training effectiveness depends on an understanding of the background and skill level of the training audience. For example, technical training provided to an audience of systems analysts and programmers will have a different level of effect than that provided to an audience of accountants. Basic demographic data may be collected at either course commencement or conclusion, but information regarding the learners' satisfaction with the course and course material should be collected at the end of the course.

Level 2: Behavior Objective Testing (Learning and Teaching Effectiveness)

This level of evaluation measures how much information or skill was transmitted from the training activity to the learner. The evaluation should be in various formats relative to the level of training. In an IT Security Basics and Literacy course, for example, participants could be given a pre-test and a post-test of multiple choice items or fill-in-the-blank statements. At an intermediate or advanced training level, participants should be given some sort of performance test, such as a case study to solve. At the education level, essay questions exploring concepts would be appropriate. The evaluation format must relate back to the behavioral objectives of the learning activity which, in turn, drive the content being presented. The Level 2 evaluation also provides instant feedback, but it is more objective than a Level 1 evaluation: it assesses how much the student remembered or demonstrated by skill performance by the end of the program—not how he/she felt about it. As previously noted, Level 2 evaluation can be built into each block of instruction and does not need to wait until the end of a course.

A Level 2 evaluation measures success in transference of information and skills to the student. It enables the evaluator to determine if a given student may need to repeat the course, or perhaps attend a different type of learning activity presenting the same material in a different format. The evaluator should be able to see if a pattern of transference problems emerges, and determine whether or not the course itself may need to be reconfigured or perhaps dropped from an organization's training program.

Behavior objective testing is possibly the most difficult measurement area to address. It is relatively easy to test the knowledge level of the attendees after completing a course or block of instruction but it is not easy to determine when that learning took place. An attendee may have had knowledge of the subject area before receiving the instruction so that the course had little or no impact. Thus, information collected solely at the conclusion of a course/instructional block must be examined relative to the attendee's background and education.

To better determine the learning impact of a specific course or instructional block, an approach is to use pre/post testing in which testing is performed at the outset, and the results are compared to testing conducted at the conclusion of instruction.

Testing of an attendee's knowledge of a particular subject area by including questions or tasks where there is a single right answer or approach is appropriate for almost all testing situations, especially at the beginning and intermediate levels. Questions regarding selection of the "best" answer among possible options should be reserved for those training environments where there is opportunity for analysis regarding why a particular answer is better than other answers.

Level 3: Job Transfer Skills (Student Performance Effectiveness)

This evaluation is the first level which asks for more than student input. At this level, the evaluator, through a structured questionnaire usually administered 30 to 60 days following the training activity, asks the supervisor about the performance of the employee(s) relative to the behavioral objectives of the course. This is a "before" and "after" job skills comparison. In some cases this information is difficult to obtain, especially when employees' job functions and grade levels permit them considerable autonomy, without direct supervision. When supervisors observe only the final output of employee actions, developing a valid questionnaire can present a particular challenge. When accomplished successfully, a Level 3 evaluation should begin to show the extent to which the learning activity benefits the organization as well as the employee.

Questions appropriate for the learner's supervisor might include:

- Has the learner used the knowledge obtained in the course to accomplish job tasks?

- Has the learner's performance improved since taking the course?

Level 4: Organizational Benefit (Training Program Effectiveness)

Level 4 evaluations can be difficult to undertake and hard to quantify. They can involve structured, follow-up interviews with students, their supervisors, and colleagues. They can

Information Technology Security Training Requirements

involve comparison by a subject-matter expert of outputs produced by a student both before and after training. They can involve some form of benchmarking, or evaluation of the particular training activity in relation to other options for a particular job performance measure. In all cases they involve quantifying the value of resulting improvement in relation to the cost of training. Level 4 evaluations, properly designed, can help senior management officials to answer such hypothetical questions as: "Is it more cost-effective to devote limited training resources to the education of a single, newly-appointed IT security specialist in this organization, or to devote the same resources to security basics and literacy training of all employees in the organization?"; or "Is it a better return on investment to train 'front-end' systems designers and developers in building security rules commensurate with the sensitivity of the system, or to train 'back-end' users in compliance with currently existing system rules?" Determination of the purpose and objectives of a Level 4 evaluation, as well as the number of variables and the method of measurement of skill level, should only be done following completion of Level 3 evaluation(s), utilizing the findings thereof.

5.4 Implementation of Evaluation Planning

The information in Exhibit 5-1 should help in starting a comprehensive evaluation effort of an organization's IT security training program. Each cell suggests the overall skill objective which should be attained by the cell evaluator (e.g., instructor, or the student's supervisor, as appropriate) and/or the overall program evaluator with respect to the various types of learning programs. Each cell also produces a variety of specific information and requires different tools.

Because of the vast amount of data collected, evaluation tools usually consist of a series of questions which require response on a Likert-type scale. This scale, from one to five (one being very good; five being not good, or vice versa), allows the evaluator to prioritize the usefulness of the overall training program and the specific courses or learning events or components within it. Each tool is program- and site-specific.

A practical method to use is to choose a starting point in Exhibit 5-1, beginning with a type of training the organization currently offers; then find an evaluation tool appropriate to a cell at that level and borrow or adapt the concepts presented from already-developed tools. Samples of some of these evaluation tools appear as Exhibits 5-2 and 5-3. Agency training staff may be able to help locate other tools.

(Text continues after exhibits, on page 170.)

Exhibit 5-1
Evaluation Objectives

Levels of Evaluation → Type of Training ↘	Level 1: Student Satisfaction	Level 2: Learning Effectiveness	Level 3: Performance Effectiveness	Level 4: Training Program Effectiveness
Basics/Literacy	How well did the student think he/she grasped the security concepts? For CBT, how many attempts did it take for the student to pass the test?	How did the majority of students perform on the test, e.g., do aggregated post-test answers show sufficient improvement over pre-test answers?	How well is the student using the core skill set in his or her daily activities routinely?	Did the number and severity of security incidents go down as a result? Did the cost of security compliance go down? If so, how much?
Training	How well did the training program fit the student's expectations?	Did the training program demonstrably and sufficiently increase the scope and/or depth of the student's skill set?	How well is the student applying the new security skills to functional job requirements?	Did the number and severity of security incidents go down as a result? Did the cost of security compliance go down? If so, how much?
Education	Did the course of study advance the student's career development or professional qualifications in IT security?	Could the student apply the increased knowledge to a real-world situation adequately?	How well is the student's acquired IT security knowledge being used to advance agency goals & objectives?	Did the number and severity of security incidents go down as a result? Did the cost of security compliance go down? If so, how much?

Information Technology Security Training Requirements

**Exhibit 5-2
Sample Questionnaire — Level 1 Evaluation
Training Assessment by Student**

1. Indicate your highest level of education:

    ○ High School graduate or less
    ○ Some college/technical school
    ○ Associate degree or technical certification
    ○ Bachelor's Degree
    ○ Master's Degree
    ○ Doctorate

2. Indicate the total number of courses you have completed in subject areas related to this training:

    ○ 0
    ○ 1-4
    ○ 5-10
    ○ 11-15
    ○ More than 15

3. Indicate how long it has been since you took a course in the subject area of this training:

    ○ This is my first course in this subject
    ○ Less than 1 year
    ○ 1-3 years
    ○ 4-6 years
    ○ More than 6 years

4. Indicate the extent of your work experience in the general subject areas of this training:

    ○ None
    ○ Less than 1 year
    ○ 1-3 years
    ○ 4-6 years
    ○ More than 6 years

5. For my preparation and level of knowledge, the training was:

    ○ Too elementary
    ○ Somewhat elementary
    ○ Somewhat difficult
    ○ Too difficult
    ○ About right

6. The pace at which the subject matter was covered was:

    ○ Too slow
    ○ Somewhat slow
    ○ Somewhat fast
    ○ Too fast
    ○ About right

7. For what I got out of this training, the workload was:

    ○ Light
    ○ About right
    ○ Heavy

8. Considering my previous experience with this subject matter, the course content was:

    ○ Out of date
    ○ Somewhat current
    ○ Current
    ○ State-of-the-art
    ○ Not applicable (no previous experience)

Continued on next page.

Information Technology Security Training Requirements

Exhibit 5-2 (Continued) Sample Questionnaire — Level 1 Evaluation Training Assessment by Student

9. Which of the following best describes the usefulness of this training for your job:

   ○ Not particularly useful   ○ Very useful
   ○ Somewhat useful   ○ Essential

10. How much did you learn from this training:

    ○ Not much
    ○ A moderate amount
    ○ A great deal

Student Perception of Instructor

Extent to which the instructor successfully:	Excellent	Good	Fair	Poor	N/A
1. Presented material in an organized manner					
2. Communicated knowledge of the subject matter					
3. Made difficult concepts understandable					
4. Used class time effectively					
5. Stimulated interest in the subject area					
6. Demonstrated positive attitude toward participants					
7. Overall, I would rate this instructor					

Student Perception of Course Quality

Course content:	Excellent	Good	Fair	Poor	N/A
1. Clarity of course objectives					
2. Agreement between course objectives and course content					
3. Agreement between Tests/Exams and course objectives					
4. Degree to which the organization of the course enhanced my					
5. Opportunities to practice/apply course content during					
6. Effectiveness of textbook(s), handouts, or other material					
7. Quality of classroom/lab facilities					
8. Overall, I would rate this course					

Chapter 5. Evaluating Training Effectiveness

Information Technology Security Training Requirements

**Exhibit 5-3
Sample Questionnaire — Level 3 Evaluation
Training Assessment by Supervisor**

SECTION I - COURSE RELATION TO JOB REQUIREMENTS

1. What was the chief reason for nominating the employee for this course?

   ○ Information is required in present job
   ○ Information is required in new job
   ○ Course provides prerequisite or background for other training
   ○ Course is required to meet certification
   ○ Course provides general career development
   ○ Other (please specify) _____

2. Considering past experience/training and present/future job assignments, how well timed was this course in the employee's career?

   ○ Took before needed
   ○ Took when needed
   ○ Needed course earlier, but wasn't offered
   ○ Needed course earlier, but couldn't get in
   ○ Didn't need course and probably will never use it
   ○ Unable to assess at this time

3. Which of the following best describes the usefulness of this training for the employee's job?

   ○ Essential
   ○ Very useful
   ○ Somewhat useful
   ○ Not particularly useful
   ○ Unable to assess at this time

4. How frequently does the employee need the skills or knowledge acquired in this course?

   ○ Daily
   ○ Weekly
   ○ Periodically
   ○ Not currently used, but needed for background or future use
   ○ Criteria does not apply to this course

Continued on next page.

Chapter 5. Evaluating Training Effectiveness

Exhibit 5-3 (Continued)
Sample Questionnaire — Level 3 Evaluation
Training Assessment by Supervisors

SECTION II - COURSE IMPACT ON EMPLOYEE PERFORMANCE

Rate the degree to which the employee's IT security-related job performance was affected by the training in this course.

Job Impact	1	2	3	4	5
Knowledge of IT security-related job duties					
Technical skills (include applicable language-related skills)					
Productivity					
Accuracy					
Use of job aids (e.g., reference aids, software applications)					
Overall work quality					

Legend:
1 = Greatly improved   3 = Moderately improved   5 = Not applicable
2 = First-time impact   4 = No change

SECTION III - RETURN ON TRAINING INVESTMENT

1. How would you describe the trade-off between the employee's time away from the job versus IT security-related benefits from taking this course?

    ○ Great benefits from training offset employee time away from the job
    ○ Modest benefits from training offset employee time away from the job
    ○ Benefits from training did not offset employee time away from the job
    ○ Do not have enough information to respond
    ○ Benefits from this course can not be measured in this manner

2. How would you respond if another employee from your area needed/wanted to take this course?

    ○ Would definitely nominate others if I knew the course was applicable to their duties
    ○ Would not nominate others because _____
    ○ Would nominate others only if the following course changes were made:
    _____
    _____

    ○ Do not have enough information to decide.

Continued on next page.

Information Technology Security Training Requirements

Exhibit 5-3 (Continued)
Sample Questionnaire — Level 3 Evaluation
Training Assessment by Supervisor

3. How knowledgeable were you about the course content before receiving this form?

   ○ I had read the catalog description or brochure and knew the expected behavioral outcome.

   ○ I had read the catalog description or brochure but did not know the expected behavioral outcome.

   ○ I knew the overall purpose or goal of the course but did not read a detailed description of it and did not know the expected behavioral outcome.

   ○ I only knew the course existed.

   ○ I knew nothing about the course until I received this form.

4. As a supervisor, how satisfied are you with the training results from this course?

   ○ Highly satisfied
   ○ Satisfied
   ○ Dissatisfied
   ○ Highly dissatisfied
   ○ Unsure

Chapter 5. Evaluating Training Effectiveness

5.5 Summary

Evaluation is undertaken to measure the effectiveness of an agency's or organization's IT security training program, i.e., the extent to which the overall program and its respective components are either meaningful or a waste of the organization's limited training resources. The employee (student) must be asked their view of each learning event (Level 1 and Level 2), the supervisor their view of the event (Level 3), and the organization its view of the event (Level 4) in relation to return on investment. In this process, both quantitative and qualitative data will be collected. At Levels 3 and 4, data collection will be longitudinal. As important as it is for the evaluator to collect the raw data, analysis and application of the collected data is where the IT Security Program Manager and senior officials get the organization's money's worth out of its IT security training program. Evaluation planning in advance of the event(s) to be evaluated is essential.

To assist in this regard, Exhibit 5-4 on the following page illustrates and correlates the elements of training effectiveness evaluation that have been discussed in this chapter, i.e., the four purposes of evaluation and four types of data needed for measurement (from section 5.2), the three behavioral objectives (from subsection 5.3.1), and the four levels of evaluation (from subsection 5.3.2) along with the evaluation tools or instruments associated with each level (from section 5.4).

5.6 Chapter References

For further information about training evaluation tools, the following resources are suggested as a point of departure. This is not an exhaustive listing.

Carnevale, A.P., and Schultz, E.R. "Return on Investment: Accounting for Training," Training and Development Journal, 1990, 44 (7).

Kirkpatrick, D. "Evaluation of Training," in R. Craig (ed.), Training and Development Handbook, Third Edition. New York: McGraw-Hill, 1987.

Mitchell, K.D. Return on Investment: A Model and an Assessment of the U.S. Office of Personnel Management's Research into Evaluating Federal Training Programs, Washington, D.C.: U.S. Office of Personnel Management, 1993.

Exhibit 5-4
Correlation of Evaluation Elements

Purpose — to measure	Data Needed for Measurement	Required to Plan Evaluations	Levels of Evaluation/ Type of Evaluation Tool
Learner Satisfaction	• Data to assess conditions for learning and student subjective learning assessment	Written behavioral objectives: • Conditions of activity • Activity to be performed • Level of success	Level 1 - End of Course Evaluations • Likert-scale forms
Learning/Teaching Effectiveness (What a student has learned)	• Data to measure objectively how much knowledge/ skill was transmitted to the learner	Written behavioral objectives: • Conditions of activity • Activity to be performed • Level of success	Level 2 - Behavior Objective Testing • Pre-test/post-test • Performance test (e.g., case study) • Essay questions
Job Performance Effectiveness (Pattern of student behavioral outcomes)	• Trend data for trainer improvement	Identified steps for trend data gathering, evaluation, and extrapolation	Level 3 - Job Transfer Skills Supervisor assessment - structured questionnaire for supervisor for "before and after" skills comparison
Program Effectiveness (Value of training event compared to other options)	• Return on investment data for optimal resource allocation	Mission-related goals tied to explicit learning objectives	Level 4 - Organizational Benefit • Structured follow-up interviews with students, supervisors, and colleagues • Comparison of student outputs (before and after training) • Benchmarking

Chapter 5. Evaluating Training Effectiveness

Information Technology Security Training Requirements

INDEX

Information Technology Security Training Requirements

Index

ABC's .... vii, 27-39
Accreditation 51, 119, 121, 133, 145
Acquire 9, 28, 43, 61, 62, 75, 76, 85, 86, 97, 98, 107, 108, 127, 128, 139, 140
Acquisition/development/installation/implementation controls 36, 37
Adult learning .... v, 9, 20
Audit 28, 29, 39, 52, 53, 63, 65
Auditor, external 47, 67, 81, 91, 101, 113, 121, 133, 145, 153
Auditor, internal 47, 63, 67, 79, 81, 91, 101, 113, 121, 133, 145, 153
Authorization 29, 53
Availability 3, 27-29, 35, 36, 50
Awareness .. iii, v, 3, 5, 7, 9, 13-15, 18, 25-27, 30, 36, 37, 43, 52, 68, 74, 78, 80, 82, 84, 90, 92, 102, 137, 138, 144, 146, 158

Behavioral objectives .... vi, 159-162, 170, 171

Certification 16, 38, 47, 51, 67, 113, 119, 121, 133, 145, 165, 167
Certification reviewer 47, 67, 113, 119, 121, 133, 145
Chief Information Officer .... iv, 47, 59, 77, 79, 83, 87, 133
Computer Security Act 3, 30, 43, 59, 69
Confidentiality 3, 27, 29, 35, 36, 50, 53
Contracting Officer 47, 61, 85, 97, 107, 127, 139
Core set of It security terms and concepts .... v, 26
COTR 47, 61, 75, 85, 97, 107, 127, 139
Curriculum 8, 9, 26, 32, 33

DAA 27, 28, 38, 47, 113, 121, 133, 145
Data Center Manager 47, 111, 137, 149, 151
Database Administrator 47, 111, 119, 129, 131, 143, 149, 151
Design and develop 9, 43, 117
Designated Approving Authority 47, 113, 119, 121, 133, 145
Development ... iv-7, 9, 16, 25, 33, 36, 37, 41, 43, 44, 46, 48, 51, 52, 62-64, 68, 73, 74, 76-80, 82, 84, 86-88, 90, 92, 95-103, 105-123, 125-135, 137-147, 149, 151, 153, 158, 159, 164, 167, 170

Education . iii-6, 9, 13, 14, 16-21, 26, 43, 52, 68, 74, 78, 80, 82, 84, 90, 92, 102, 138, 144, 146, 158, 161-165
Evaluation vi-6, 9, 38, 44, 50, 61, 67, 81, 91, 157-171

Freedom of Information Act Official 47, 109

Implement and operate 9, 43

Index   I-3

Implementation . vi, 9, 31, 36-38, 43, 44, 51, 62-65, 68, 74-76, 78-80, 82-92, 95-103, 105-115, 117-123, 125-147, 149, 151, 153, 163
Individual accountability 27, 29, 34, 37, 39, 51, 69
Information Resources Management Official, Senior 47
Information Resources Manager . . 47, 59, 63, 67, 69, 73, 75, 77, 79, 83, 85, 89, 95, 101, 105, 125, 153
Information sharing . . 34, 49, 62, 64, 68, 74, 76, 78, 82, 84, 90, 92, 96, 98, 100, 102, 106, 110, 112, 120, 122, 126, 130, 132, 138, 142, 150, 152, 154
Initiation 37, 44
Integrity 3, 27, 29, 31, 35, 36, 50, 53
IT security basics and literacy 5, 9, 25, 161
IT security body of knowledge topics and concepts . . . . vii, 9, 46, 48-53
IT Security Officer/Manager 47
IT security program 7-9, 17, 26, 29, 34, 43, 48, 60, 64, 73-92, 96, 98, 100, 102, 104, 110, 170

Job function vi-6, 10, 26, 27, 29, 30, 37, 39, 46, 47

KSAs . . . . iii, 43, 44

Laws and regulations . . . . . v, 27, 30, 33, 43, 48, 57, 59, 60, 62-70, 74, 82, 84, 86, 90, 92, 150, 154
Learning continuum . . . . v-vii, 9, 11, 13, 16, 17, 19, 25, 43, 44
Learning styles . . . . v, 9, 19
Levels of evaluation . . . . vi, 6, 160, 170, 171
Life cycle security . . . . v, 9, 93, 95-101, 103, 105-154
Likert Scale 161

Manage . . . iii, 27, 31, 43, 51, 59, 60, 73, 74, 83, 84, 95, 96, 105, 106, 125, 126, 137, 138, 149, 150
Management . . 3, 4, 7, 8, 16, 27, 31, 35, 36, 38, 39, 43, 45, 47, 48, 50-52, 59-63, 65-70, 73, 74, 78, 80-92, 95, 96, 102-106, 109, 110, 112, 114, 116, 120-122, 124-126, 130, 134, 136-138, 140, 142, 144, 146, 148-154, 157, 160, 163, 170
Management controls 36, 51, 62
Model . . . . 1, iii, v, 6, 7, 9, 11, 13, 14, 26, 27, 30, 37, 43, 44

Network Administrator 47, 65, 89, 111, 119, 129, 131, 137, 141, 143, 151

Operational controls 36, 38, 52
Operations 28, 31, 38, 44, 47, 65, 89
Organization and IT Security 33

Performance-based . . . . 1, iii, 6, 7, 9

Planning vi-7, 9, 32, 36, 38, 49, 51, 52, 73-82, 101, 158, 163, 170
Privacy Act Official 47, 109, 151
Program Manager . . 16, 17, 47, 63, 73, 83, 89, 95, 99, 113, 125, 127, 129, 133, 137, 139, 149, 151, 170
Programmer/Systems Analyst 47, 63, 65, 109, 117, 119, 129, 141, 151

Records Management Official 47, 109, 151, 153
Results-based learning . . . . v, 5
Review 7, 9, 43, 47, 51, 65, 67-69, 73, 81-83, 85, 91, 92, 101, 102, 105, 109, 113, 114, 121, 122, 127, 133, 134, 139, 145, 146, 153, 154
Review and evaluate 9, 43, 113, 133
Risk management . 4, 27, 31, 35, 36, 50, 60, 62, 66, 68, 74, 78, 80, 82, 84, 88, 90, 92, 102-104, 106, 110, 114, 120, 142, 144, 146, 150, 152, 154, 160
Roles and responsibilities 3, 5, 9, 27, 37, 43, 51
Role-based training . . . . v, 9, 16, 25, 33, 41, 43
Rules of behavior 34, 37, 51

Security basics . . . . v, 5, 9, 16, 23, 25, 26, 43, 46, 161, 163
Security literacy 25, 26, 158
Security responsibility 46
Sensitivity . 3, 15, 35, 50, 51, 62, 64, 68, 74, 78, 82, 84, 90, 92, 96, 98, 100, 102, 104, 106, 110, 116, 134, 136, 150, 152, 154, 163
Separation of duties 27, 29, 37, 39, 51
Source Selection Board Member 47, 61, 75, 85, 107
System Administrator 47, 65, 89, 111, 119, 129, 131, 137, 141, 143, 151
System Designer/Developer 47, 63, 95, 97, 99, 105, 109, 111, 117, 129, 141
System environment 49, 62, 64, 68, 74, 76, 78, 82, 84, 86, 90, 92, 98, 100, 102, 110, 112, 120, 122, 126, 130, 132, 134, 142
System interconnection . 34, 49, 64, 68, 74, 76, 78, 82, 84, 90, 92, 98, 100, 102, 106, 110, 112, 120, 122, 126, 130, 132, 134, 138, 142
System Owner 47, 69, 73, 89, 95, 97, 99, 101, 103, 105, 107, 113, 121, 123, 125, 127, 133, 137, 139, 149
Systems Operations Personnel 47, 65, 129, 131, 141, 151

Technical controls 34, 36, 39, 53
Technical Support Personnel 47, 65, 111, 131, 143, 151
Telecommunications Specialist 47, 75, 143
Termination 38, 44
Test and evaluation 38
Training . . . 1, iii, v-vii, 3-10, 13-20, 25-27, 29-33, 36, 37, 41, 43-47, 52, 55, 57, 59-71, 73-93, 95-155, 157-171
Training assessment . . . . vii, 165-169
Training effectiveness . . . . vi, 8, 9, 157-159, 161, 170

Training effectiveness evaluation .... **vi, 158, 170**

User **15, 28, 29, 34, 37-39, 47, 53, 69, 103, 115, 123, 135, 147**

NIST *Technical Publications*

Periodical

Journal of Research of the National Institute of Standards and Technology—Reports NIST research and development in those disciplines of the physical and engineering sciences in which the Institute is active. These include physics, chemistry, engineering, mathematics, and computer sciences. Papers cover a broad range of subjects, with major emphasis on measurement methodology and the basic technology underlying standardization. Also included from time to time are survey articles on topics closely related to the Institute's technical and scientific programs. Issued six times a year.

Nonperiodicals

Monographs—Major contributions to the technical literature on various subjects related to the Institute's scientific and technical activities.

Handbooks—Recommended codes of engineering and industrial practice (including safety codes) developed in cooperation with interested industries, professional organizations, and regulatory bodies.

Special Publications—Include proceedings of conferences sponsored by NIST, NIST annual reports, and other special publications appropriate to this grouping such as wall charts, pocket cards, and bibliographies.

National Standard Reference Data Series—Provides quantitative data on the physical and chemical properties of materials, compiled from the world's literature and critically evaluated. Developed under a worldwide program coordinated by NIST under the authority of the National Standard Data Act (Public Law 90-396). NOTE: The Journal of Physical and Chemical Reference Data (JPCRD) is published bimonthly for NIST by the American Chemical Society (ACS) and the American Institute of Physics (AIP). Subscriptions, reprints, and supplements are available from ACS, 1155 Sixteenth St., NW, Washington, DC 20056.

Building Science Series—Disseminates technical information developed at the Institute on building materials, components, systems, and whole structures. The series presents research results, test methods, and performance criteria related to the structural and environmental functions and the durability and safety characteristics of building elements and systems.

Technical Notes—Studies or reports which are complete in themselves but restrictive in their treatment of a subject. Analogous to monographs but not so comprehensive in scope or definitive in treatment of the subject area. Often serve as a vehicle for final reports of work performed at NIST under the sponsorship of other government agencies.

Voluntary Product Standards—Developed under procedures published by the Department of Commerce in Part 10, Title 15, of the Code of Federal Regulations. The standards establish nationally recognized requirements for products, and provide all concerned interests with a basis for common understanding of the characteristics of the products. NIST administers this program in support of the efforts of private-sector standardizing organizations.

Order the **following** *NIST publications—FIPS and NISTIRs—from the National Technical Information Service, Springfield, VA 22161.*

Federal Information Processing Standards Publications (FIPS PUB)—Publications in this series collectively constitute the Federal Information Processing Standards Register. The Register serves as the official source of information in the Federal Government regarding standards issued by NIST pursuant to the Federal Property and Administrative Services Act of 1949 as amended, Public Law 89-306 (79 Stat. 1127), and as implemented by Executive Order 11717 (38 FR 12315, dated May 11, 1973) and Part 6 of Title 15 CFR (Code of Federal Regulations).

NIST Interagency or Internal Reports (NISTIR)—The series includes interim or final reports on work performed by NIST for outside sponsors (both government and nongovernment). In general, initial distribution is handled by the sponsor; public distribution is handled by sales through the National Technical Information Service, Springfield, VA 22161, in hard copy, electronic media, or microfiche form. NISTIR's may also report results of NIST projects of transitory or limited interest, including those that will be published subsequently in more comprehensive form.